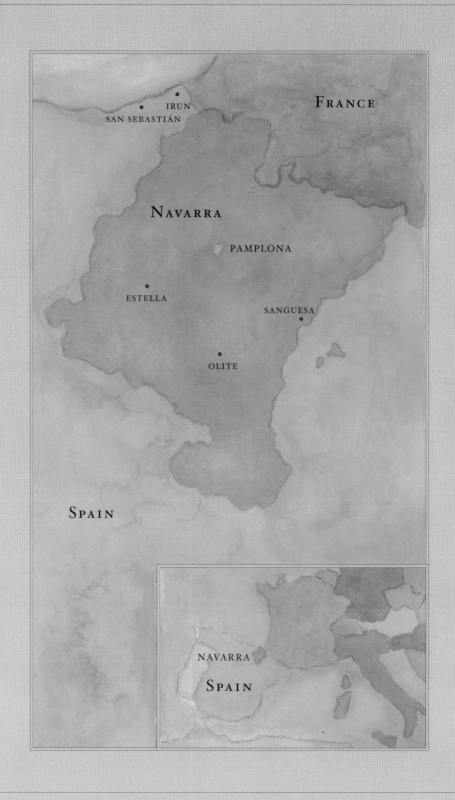

PAMPLONA

RUNNING THE BULLS, BARS AND BARRIOS IN FIESTA DE SAN FERMÍN

FIRST EDITION

ISBN 0-9721223-0-3

Published by Quinn Publishing, New Orleans
Design by Megan Barra
Printed in China

"It was hard to put down. The drama, tension, colors and sound put one in the encierro so immediately that he becomes one of the runners. Ray Mouton knows fiesta well - the sight of it, the feel of it, the smell of it, the noise of it - and the music. From the sound of a single guitar being played under the balcony of a hotel before the first bullrun to the last thump of a peña drum on the ninth day, Mouton has experienced it. The writing is great."

- ERNEST J. GAINES, author of *A Lesson Before Dying*

"Ray Mouton's love and knowledge of Spain's great 'running the bulls' fiesta is vividly reflected in this book, a rollicking 'dance in anarchy' as well as a thoughtful meditation of life and death."

- CURTIS WILKIE, author of *Dixie*

"I hadn't read but five pages before I had promised myself that I will be among the revelers on my next trip to Europe. In Pamplona, I will raise a glass - or two - in Ray Mouton's honor for making me want to get there."

- TYLER BRIDGES, Pulitzer winning journalist
and author of *Bad Bet on The Bayou*

"This book triumphs as it conveys the whole of fiesta in a way no other book has ever done. And, yes, that includes Hemingway. Reading this book you'll hear the rockets, drums, shoe shiners, metal chairs, hooves, pipes, prayers, laughter, bar talk and musical madness that forms the audible wallpaper of fiesta. It's all here. He's nailed the damn thing down. It's a beautiful book, a victorious work."

-EAMONN O'NEILL, author of *Matadors: A Journey in the Heart of Modern Bullfighting*

"This is the definitive work on Sanfermines. I could not put it down. This book makes the true cultural, ethnic, historical essence, spirit and significance of fiesta accessible to readers all over the world. I am grateful to Ray Mouton for having written this true and engaging picture of one of Spain's most endearing and glorious Fiestas."

- MURIEL FEINER, author of *La Mujer en el Mundo Del Toro*

PAMPLONA

RUNNING THE BULLS, BARS AND BARRIOS IN FIESTA DE SAN FERMÍN

RAY MOUTON

QUINN PUBLISHING

New Orleans

In Memory of Matador John Fulton
whose life was a fiesta

And for my brother John Mouton
whose life is a fiesta.

"Pamplona is the last legal drug ...
a delirium that doesn't stop, a
communion with absurdity."

CARMEN RIGALT, *EL RUEDO*

"You give of yourself when you run the bulls ... you let it all go ... your time, your money, your belief, your life, your self, into the wild forms of joy and fiesta."

LEGENDARY BULLRUNNER MATT CARNEY

LA FIESTA

PAMPLONA'S FIESTA is the last remaining stop on the romantic road. Those who gather here each year dance to their own drummer. The drumbeat they hear is not so different as it is distant. It is a faint rhythm which the romantic hears all year long; a soft, strong sound which is never heard by others, much like the heartbeat of a lover long asleep in your arms.

This ancient city in the foothills of the Pyrenees Mountains with its high stone ramparts and walled citadel transforms each July to a place where the nights are never ending and the mornings majestic, as noble creatures, beasts of mythology made by a patient God, race through the streets for a brief moment ordering the whole universe, creating an energy field unlike any other on earth.

Fiesta has accurately been described as one of the most exhilarating experiences on earth. All a book can capture are images and impressions because the event is an elusive, metaphysical experience that nearly defies description. All of Fiesta is about the heart, the *alegría* or joy flowing from the generous spirit of those who call this enchanted country, once the Kingdom of

OPPOSITE PAGE: *The rural high country of Navarra, a pastoral landscape that is often partially obscured by mountain mist and sometimes shrouded in clouds, provides a dramatic backdrop for the city of Pamplona where Fiesta plays out.*

Navarra, their home.

This ancient kingdom spread across the Pyrenees Mountains into France. This Basque country is a land apart, one of the most beautiful landscapes on earth. With images this book will show some of the Basque country which cradles the cities, villages, castles, churches, vineyards and farms of the region. It is from this land and these people that this Fiesta was born. The grandeur of this land provides a lush backdrop for the beauty of Fiesta.

When Fiesta is over, an impression is all it leaves. The moments fold into one's memory like a kaleidoscope. For nine days beginning on the sixth of July you experience an incomparable and unrelenting sensory bombardment. The impressions that remain when the celebration is over hang in your head and heart the way wisps of white smoke linger in the sky when rockets fire from the town hall signaling the beginning and end of the celebration.

Some of the impressions you are left with are vivid while others are vague. Many memories are faded like an old black and white photograph while other recollections are brightly colored. And some of what you feel you remember is only what you imagine.

During Fiesta drummers are always near. The drummers never tire. When Fiesta's final act is finished, at dawn following the last night, the musicians head home. Some march under the old stone arch, an ancient gateway to the city, strolling in loose formation down a steep hill across a bridge over the Arga river. As they go into the distance, fading into the dawn, their instruments go silent but occasionally one drum continues to sound. If you hear this drummer after he has faded from view and gone off into the dawn, then the sound of this distant drummer will beat within you for a year, until this time comes again.

PAMPLONA

Running the Bulls, Bars and Barrios
in Fiesta de San Fermín

T HE SUN RISES OVER PAMPLONA gently, lighting this northern corner of Spain with a fragile first light. Dawn approaches
Pamplona subtly and slowly. In summer, on the seventh day of the
seventh month, early sunlight is shielded by the Pyrenees
Mountains which divide Spain from France. The jagged peaks filter
out all brightness, painting the sky pastel blue.

During the morning, as the sunlight becomes brighter it will
create shadows on stone streets and plazas, soft silhouettes of tow-
ers, turrets and steeples. By midday, after the shadows recede, the
city will wear a crown – a bright blue cupola like those found over
royal residences and great cathedrals. The horizon will seem to
begin and end with the old walls of the city. For the next eight days
all that matters in the world will seem to exist only here.

At dawn on the seventh there is only a hint of what is to come.
This soft light is only a faint allusion to the bright illumination of
Fiesta which will make it difficult to distinguish night from day. For a
total of nine days Pamplona is a place of many rituals, but few rules.
As this dawn approaches the first day of Fiesta has already passed.
This, the seventh day of the seventh month, is the day of the Saint.

Standing on a balcony in the oldest barrio at sunrise on July 7 is
like watching the lighting of an antique painting. As the curtain of

The sun rises over the Pyrenees and Pamplona.

darkness is drawn, old stone buildings and narrow cobblestone streets worn and weathered through the ages reveal themselves. Everything around me is of another time, anchored in antiquity.

Pamplona is near a site where Romans camped nearly a hundred years before the birth of Christ. There are places around the world older than Pamplona, but this morning Pamplona seems ageless, with a story as long as any city in the world. Even before the first people wandered over this site, before the first encampment was built here, Pamplona existed. It lived through the early ages as a feeling without locale, patiently waiting to be physically born. Even today, especially today, Pamplona is more an emotion than a place.

I hear a song from the street beneath this balcony and the tune takes me back to the present. A Bob Dylan song drifts up from the guitar of a Spanish boy in the street below. He has been there all night. First, he was with friends and they sang old folk songs in Spanish, then they sang a Beatle harmony in English. Now he stands alone, strumming a song about struggle. A heavy metal band played in one of the plazas last night, a big band in another, and somewhere I recall hearing Neil Young's soaring guitar feedback reverberating from a small bar on a crowded street. This modern music cuts

6

across the medieval ambience, blurring time, overlaying the past with the present. This is the beginning of the twenty-first century, yet there remain traces of the two thousand years of Roman, Alani, Vandal, Suevian, Visigoth and Basque history that happened here. The past and present peacefully co-exist with the past dominating the mood of one moment and then graciously giving way to the present in the next.

During Fiesta wandering bands of musicians will play ancient tunes and strong male voices will spontaneously sing songs of the province, *jotas*, music which has its origin in distant eras. But most of last night the old stone walls echoed rock'n'roll.

Though this marathon celebration is less than 24 hours old, the street below is already getting messy. In the days which follow, some streets will be covered with the debris of celebration, resembling the site of a battlefield rout. The real heroes of the Fiesta are not matadors who are carried out of the bullring on the shoulders of the crowd or bullrunners who are acclaimed for their bravery and artistry in the morning *encierro*, but rather the municipal workers who hose down the streets and collect the garbage. They are out-numbered ten thousand to one by revelers, yet they perform in a commendable manner during the early part of the week until the weekend crowd overwhelms them.

Pamplona is home to approximately a quarter-million resi-dents, and that number will more than triple during Fiesta. On the weekend nearest July 14, Bastille Day, the French will invade, streaming across the Pyrenees, swelling the crowd to a point which outstrips the capacity of the city in every respect. There will be too many bullrunners in the morning, too many standing in line for food in the evening and some streets will be impassable, forcing revelers to dance in place. Many will sleep in the parks, in doorways, and even in the streets themselves. The lucky ones will sleep in chairs or on benches for the streets will be filthy. Though the municipal workers struggle mightily to wash down all the streets with power-ful streams of water shooting out of hand held hoses, the only streets which are sure to be washed every day are those where the

bulls run, thus these will be among the cleanest streets during Fiesta, if not the safest. These streets present an obvious danger for a few minutes each morning and a less obvious danger in the evening. One is not safe in these streets even at night. Several years ago a street-cleaning truck hit a reveler slumbering against a curb, chewed him up and killed him.

I remember that event and other ugly incidents I have experienced, witnessed or heard about during past Fiestas, and I know all about the dirt, the garbage and smells that come with Fiesta. I also know how massive crowds following or leading bands through narrow streets can involuntarily become a cruel and unforgiving mass, their clothes wet with wine and grime. I know how it feels and smells to slam head-on into such a parade. I know about these things and I push them from my mind because I also know there will be great beauty in Fiesta and beauty will conquer all.

On this first morning of Fiesta, no ugly recollections of Fiestas past can compete with the romance of the present. As I look down into the street, both my hands grip the old, iron balcony rail. I realize that this railing may well be the last thing I have a firm grip on for the next eight days. I let go.

THIS balcony will be valuable each morning as it provides a ringside seat for the running of the bulls. A balcony along the route of the running is one of the few places where one can get a glimpse of the spectacle. Tonight the balcony is empty. I am alone. Behind me is a small *pensión*. I stay at a small hotel on the other side of the central plaza. I walked a friend home tonight and came out to the balcony when he retired. I've remained here for hours. Friends of mine have spent Fiesta in the same rooms of this house for years. As I came out to the balcony I noticed lights in two of the rooms where friends live for these nine days. One is a filmmaker, the other an artist. The painter is an early riser, one who loves the early light, and I know he is now dressing for the encierro, and he will soon saunter out for a coffee on the plaza. As he

OPPOSITE PAGE: *Balconies draw a crowd as the morning gets underway.*

rises, I know the filmmaker is just turning in, finishing the night and readying for sleep. One friend runs the bulls in the morning, the other runs the bars all night, and there are some who do both. I know my friends' habits and they know mine. We are part of a loosely bound contingent of foreigners in Fiesta who some call the *cuadrilla*, foreigners who return to Fiesta year after year.

Last night I spent hours with close friends in a wonderful old restaurant that has been in the same family for generations. Dinner conversation rambled as we traded news of mutual friends: who has already arrived in town, who's due in later in the week, what our lodging arrangements are, and post-Fiesta travel plans.

Our crowd is diverse. Among our Fiesta friends are people working on the front lines in war-torn areas. Others lead sedate lives in pastoral settings in rural sections of America. A few are true expatriates who have lived outside of their homeland for many years. So many live in distant and exotic locales that it seems one of us is always near breaking news. There are a lot of writers, journalists and photographers in our midst, and a call to a friend during the year sometimes provides a private view of a conflict, a tragedy or a historic event. With cell phone technology, occasionally calls are answered with the sound of gunfire in the background. Most of these foreign correspondents and war photographers try to break off of their assignments to be in Fiesta every year. In these times of turmoil with terrorism hitting so many places with random violence, the chaos of Fiesta classifies as a respite for some of the journalists. Most of us who belong to this loosely, ill-defined crowd of foreigners first met in Pamplona. Our bond is founded in Fiesta and we return each year with feelings of reunion.

During our first Fiesta dinner, we mostly discuss news of our families and tell a few tall tales. Later, however, when Fiesta is underway, that kind of talk will give way to the things of the moment. As we live our lives in the days and nights of this magnificent masquerade honoring Saint Fermín, our own past fades from memory. All that matters is that we are here in Pamplona again.

The Spanish kid below my balcony strums his guitar and hums

what sounds like a Dylan love song. I want him to play *Tambourine Man*. Instead, he saunters away, following a group of young blondes who appear to be German or Scandinavian, possibly American. It has been a long night of adventure for all of them. They have stayed up all night. On my first Fiesta night when I was young, I did not sleep either. The first night was so good that I believed it must be the best night, and I did not want to miss a moment. Now over thirty years have passed since that first night and I did not sleep last night either.

Eight nights and days remain. Those nights and days will be welded into a singular experience, and in the end almost all memory of the experience will melt like ice on a coal stove, evaporate and disappear with no trace that it ever existed. That will happen soon enough. Now the carnival is just beginning and all things are being called to chaos rather than order. We will all dance in anarchy in the days and nights to come. We will enjoy many moments and there will be a few moments we will only be able to endure. In Fiesta one experiences almost every emotion known to the human condition.

Looking upward I see the sky becoming brighter, now giving light like a crystal chandelier gently illuminating an imaginary ballroom below, revealing dancers twirling beneath soft light. In Pamplona at dawn on the seventh day of the seventh month, there are always dancers beneath the first light, most who have forsaken sleep and have kept moving through the night. Some of them will not notice dawn until it has turned to day because of the way the blackness slowly softens to a blue hue. What they will notice is the weather. There is a saying here that at sunset the wind goes away to sleep in the mountains only to return at dawn.

Though it is mid-summer, the morning air is quite cold here in the foothills of the Pyrenees. People are sleeping on the stone floors of plazas, in the grass of parks, inside autos, propped up in alleys and in chairs at sidewalk cafés. There are no rooms at the inn, any inn. Beds in hotels, pensións and private homes are filled. Those who have been to Fiesta before arrived early and secured accommodations. Latecomers will do the best they can.

Pamplona itself is awakening from a long sleep begun when Fiesta ended a year earlier. Outside of Fiesta, for fifty weeks a year, the city is a vibrant commercial center, a town as nice as any, a place with a weekend ambiance that rivals Fiesta in certain streets. But to those who have experienced what Spaniards call *Sanfermines*, Pamplona seems shrouded in mourning the rest of the year. The morning dawn on July 7 lifts Pamplona's dark veil to reveal the brightly painted mask of the masquerade.

For Catholics the seventh is a holy day, the feast day of the

The procession of the saint in Calle Mayor on July 7.

Saint. Fermín was a Pamplona-born priest who preached the Gospel here and in Gaul. His feast day will be observed solemnly. Fermín was martyred, beheaded in the French city of Amiens in 434, and in 1186 a piece of his skull was returned to the city and liturgical celebrations were established in his honor.

A solemn moment every year when San Fermín is serenaded by Maria Cruz Corral.

On this day there will be a solemn procession from the San Lorenzo church to the center of the old quarter and back to the chapel of San Fermín on the right side of the church. The dress of those in the procession dates back centuries and the music is of another time as well. Crowds line the street for hours in certain sections, sitting on the sidewalks and eating pastries from nearby shops. They wait for the moment when the procession will stop and the idol will be serenaded by Navarran singer Maria Cruz Corral. Her voice brings tears to the eyes of locals who understand the song and monolingual foreigners are almost as moved by the sound and sight of the moment. When the singing is finished, musicians raise their guitars over their heads in a salute to the Saint as it makes its way back home.

The religious aspect of Fiesta is generally lost on the thousands of people who gather here annually only because this is the greatest party on the planet, but many Navarrans will participate in religious ceremonies and processions honoring the Saint as their ancestors have done since 1324.

The week begins and ends in ways which are both riotous and religious, sometimes at the same time. Those who follow the religious procession and hear the singing along the way may be moved by the solemnity and devotion of the faithful. They may also be amused by the rudeness some celebrants direct at unpopular political officials who join in the march through the city.

At dawn on the seventh many people have been celebrating non-stop for sixteen hours, since a rocket, the *chupinazo*, was fired from the town hall balcony at noon on the sixth announcing the commencement of the celebration. As that first rocket soars high into the sky an explosion of energy occurs on the ground when thousands break into song and spread across the city. The opening ceremony in *Plaza Consistorial* fronting the *Ayuntamiento*, the town hall, is a mob scene, the largest rugby scrum on earth. The crowd is a young, exuberant, undisciplined legion armed with an arsenal of cheap champagne that is poured and sprayed over everyone within firing range. When it is warm, the sweating crowd shouts for water from above and housewives pour buckets from balconies, drenching them as they chant, "*A-gua! A-gua! A-gua!*"

By noon on the sixth the city is filled. Local residents pour out into the plazas and crowd balconies. The population doubles and triples as traffic from across Europe crawls closer to the celebration. The bus depot and train station look like Grand Central at rush hour. Even on the outskirts of town, far from the city center, in a campground resembling a mini-Woodstock the mood shifts into

All eyes are fixed on the balcony of the town hall as thousands await the chupinazo, the firing of a rocket to open Fiesta. Pañuelos or scarves held above their heads, the whole town chants the saint's name, "San Fermín! San Fermín! San Fermín!"

high gear as backpackers from every continent scramble to line up to catch the shuttle bus or hitch a ride to the most intense celebration on earth.

The place I choose for the opening ceremony is an elegant café

A young girl and her troupe participate in a traditional Basque dance. PREVIOUS SPREAD: *In answer to their prayer-like chants, water is poured over the crowd from balconies above.*

on *Plaza del Castillo*. It too is packed an hour before noon. I choose this café because Pamplona families gather here, young children with their parents and grandparents surrounded by lifelong friends. All are dressed in traditional whites, wearing red waist sashes and holding their *pañuelos*, red scarves, above their heads. In unison, like the thousands at town hall and along the streets leading to Plaza Consistorial, they chant "*San Fer-mín! San Fer-mín! San Fer-mín!*" until the chupinazo fires. The roar of the crowd as the rocket explodes drowns out the ringing of nearby church bells sounding the hour.

The people surrounding me in the café, and so many of the people of Pamplona, are strikingly attractive. The women are like hard, smooth stones wrapped in antique lace. Their stunning beauty belies their great strength. The men are genial, gregarious. Their expressive eyes and emotional way of speaking, their body language – especially the way they use their hands for emphasis – is classically Mediterranean. The sense of family here is apparent and impressive. Almost always, husbands and wives, their parents and brothers and sisters are together, usually surrounded by young children. The people of Pamplona value this Fiesta which – despite its carnival atmosphere – is not a frivolous thing to them. Their culture, traditions and customs have great value to them, and exactly what Fiesta means to them is something a foreigner may never know. While their history may be read, their emotions cannot be exported. It is in their faces though, this very pronounced pride.

Though it will be years before he runs with the bulls, three-year old Michael Boylan already has the proper stance and the center of the street.

Sometimes it seems there are many more older people in Pamplona than in other cities of comparable size, for the elderly are very visible here, not hidden away in old folks' homes as is the case in our country. The senior citizens are almost uniform in their appearance. The men almost always wear a dark colored beret and carry a walking cane, and in the mornings the women all seem to have a small shopping bag in one hand and a long loaf of bread in the other. Equally impressive are the young children of Pamplona who seem to surround you during

the celebration. The young ones are not spectators, but participants in this grand fiesta that forms a large part of their heritage.

Fiesta, with its inconveniences for residents, drives some to their summer homes in the mountains, the homes of relatives in distant cities, or other vacation spots. But it seems almost everyone who remains in town participates in Fiesta and each family has a unique history in Fiesta with its own customs and traditions. For instance, there is the Moreno clan, owners of the historic *Hotel La Perla* on

A boy's face is filled with pride and joy as he sings a song of his culture, a jota *handed down over centuries by his ancestors.*

Plaza del Castillo. One of the Moreno brothers, Lalo, is a retired *matador* and he plays a prominent role every morning as he acts as a *doblador* at the end of the bullrun, standing in the bullring in jeans and a sweater, a matador's cape in his hands, luring the bulls away from the runners and into the corral. Lalo's brother, the affable Rafael, runs the family hotel. For many years, bulls raised on a Moreno ranch appeared in Pamplona's *plaza de toros*. Most people in Pamplona work through the week at their regular occupations and still find time to celebrate fully – they get their work done, attend vespers and mass, observe the religious processions, watch or participate in the encierros, attend bullfights, dance in the street and share endless meals with family and friends in a variety of settings.

For forty years people have spent fiesta in a small family run hotel founded by Jose Luis Eslava and his father. Located on the ancient ramparts in a narrow street across from a convent and next to a park, the unusual structure stands tall and surveys a valley below and mountains in the distance. Music is as much a part of the Eslava family traditions as bulls are part of the Moreno history. Both Jose Luis and his wife, Charo, have sung in choirs, and today their son, Eduardo, is part of the prestigious *Capilla De Musica De La Catedral De Pamplona* that opens the religious ceremonies of Sanfermines with vespers on the evening of July 6 in the San Lorenzo church. Eduardo's aunt, Carmen Eslava, participates in the liturgy on the altar. One is not likely to find any of the Eslava family engaged in the rowdy side of Sanfermines, for their fiesta and their lives are all about family, faith and music.

Except for the few minutes of the encierro each morning, *La Casa del Libro*, a bookstore and newsstand at *Estafeta* 36 is open all day long. It is a family-owned business. For the few minutes the street is closed by police and the door is locked, one of the owner's sons who is in the shop working the rest of the day is in the encierro. His name is Carmelo Butini and he usually begins his run in the lower half of Estafeta. When his luck is good, his run ends near the doorway to his shop. Carmelo runs every day and he is a historian of sorts and has an extensive collection of photographs and memorabilia about Pamplona both in and out of Fiesta, material handed down by his ancestors. Carmelo is only an example, one of thousands in Pamplona who participate in the encierro and then go straight to work. Yet, like so many others, Carmelo does not seem to miss out on anything in Fiesta. The Fiesta is part of his family's life in every sense. His brother, in fact, is named Fermín.

Clary Loinaz has been like a little sister, big sister and godmother to many of the foreigners who have been in Fiesta for years. Clary is the one many rely on to make arrangements for them in regard to major and minor details, especially any emergencies that might arise. She and her sister Miren seem to be typical of the women in the town. No one who knows them is sure when they sleep or whether they sleep at all during Fiesta. Clary was once asked by a foreigner whether she remembered her first Fiesta. She furrowed her brow and appeared confused by the query. It was not that she did not understand the language, for she is fluent in

English. It was that she did not understand the question. She smiled, shrugged and said, "There was no first Fiesta. There was always Fiesta." And so it is for the people of Pamplona. Many first attend when in the womb and return to the celebration the next year wrapped in a baby blanket, and take their first steps at the same time they are trying to dance to the music of a passing *peña* band. For them, there is always Fiesta.

ALL last night people followed the music through the streets, drifting *barrio* to barrio, neighborhood to neighborhood, bar to bar. Now they stroll quietly over the cobblestones. The morning mood is different. A lot of the people who have rambled through the night in a carefree way are beginning to be focused by their fear. Their thoughts turn to the morning encierro which will begin at eight.

Some of them are uncertain whether they will try to squeeze into one of the narrow places along the route to watch the running, buy a seat in the bullring to watch the entrance of the bulls and runners, or enter the street and run with the bulls.

In hotels, pensións, apartments and houses across the city there are some who have no questions, no doubt, for they have run with the bulls each day of Fiesta for many years. The local press refers to these bullrunners collectively as *mozos*, which literally means lads, though many are middle-aged and older. There are a large number of locals who run day after day in Fiesta, year after year, in the Navarran way, a way they call *noble y bravo,* noble and brave.

Most mozos or regular runners, natives and foreigners alike, perform a private ritual before the encierro. Some have a tradition of going to an early morning mass, a communion service attended by some of the most experienced Navarran runners. Others religiously or superstitiously always wear the same piece of clothing.

THOUGH rites involving bulls date back to man's beginnings, it was the Navarran men of Pamplona who established the ritual of running with bulls. This morning's encierro will cover the same half-mile course set in the middle eighteen-hundreds, and before that time there were other courses in Pamplona dating to the fifteen-hundreds.

The origin of the relationship between man and bull may be traced to ancient rituals recorded in cave paintings which depict a larger animal, an auroch, ancestor of the *toro bravo*, today's fighting bull. Early hunters engaged the wild, aggressive aurochs in deadly combat. The first encounters were probably matters of self-defense. Later they hunted the beast as much for its heavy, warm hide as its meat.

Primitive artists created images of these wild bulls on stone, drawings and paintings made by mixing the blood of the bull with natural preservatives, recording the deeds of hunter-heroes on cave walls. Formal bull ceremonies evolved in Europe from acrobatic events in ancient Crete through the era of royal equestrian *toreo*, bullfighting from horseback, to the modern *corridas*, bullfights of Spain, Mexico and other Hispanic cultures. Bullfighting is not something indigenous to the Iberian peninsula nor is it only practiced here today. Just as Roman emperors imported bulls from Sevilla for spectacles in the Colosseum, so do empresarios today import the best bulls to France to be fought by leading matadors in rings fashioned from ancient Roman arenas in Nimes and Arles. Throughout history in theaters of all kinds, it has been only trained professionals who encountered bulls in a formal ceremonial manner: acrobats, gladiators, royal horsemen and matadors on foot.

The first running of bulls, true encierros, began in the wild with the natural migrations of herds across the Iberian peninsula. The Moors hunted bulls from horseback, not for their meat or hides, but rather as target practice. Later, bulls of this breed began to be raised on ranches and were tended by men mounted on horseback as is the case today. Throughout time whenever ordinary men encountered fighting bulls on foot, they followed their instincts and fled. They ran *from* the bulls. Not the Navarrans.

Hundreds of years ago, men in Pamplona began to run *with* the bulls and over the years the best of them have elevated running with bulls to an art form. The running of the bulls in Pamplona began because of the bullfight. The first fights in Pamplona were held in the center of town, in what is now Plaza del Castillo. These events did not nearly resemble the bullfight as we know it today. Sometimes there were a half dozen animals in the arena at one time and even more men than that participating. With the advent of the formal ritual we are familiar with today, a bullring was built in Pamplona. The original plaza de toros and the next several structures that replaced it were all in a location different from the site of the present ring.

In most cities in Spain the bulls are herded and then transported by truck to holding corrals attached to the bullring. In Pamplona, the bulls for the corrida have always been kept in a place some distance from the site of their final act, as is the case today. Originally they were kept across the river in an open pasture on the outskirts of town, and later in corrals a long way from the arena. On the morning of a corrida the animals were herded by men on horseback to the place of the bullfight. This task remained the same for centuries. In the early morning a sound like muffled, rolling thunder would carom off the old stone walls as bull and horse hooves struck cobblestones, galloping toward the place where the pageantry would play out in the afternoon. Sometime in the fifteen hundreds some men in Pamplona joined in the encierro and ran alongside the herd. Legend goes that when none were injured, locals pointed to the heavens and exclaimed that Saint Fermín must have unfurled his cape to save them from harm. A tradition was born, and to this day the mozos still sing a prayer to the saint before each encierro, a prayer of devotion and a plea for protection. Old etchings show butchers racing on the sidewalk, wrapped in aprons, cleavers in hand, sizing up the amount of meat that would come their way once the bulls were ready to become steaks and chops. It is unlikely that butchers had anything to do with establishing the tradition of the encierro as we know it today. No one knows what kind of men ran with the bulls first. The earliest photographs only tell us something about their attire and ages. The first runners were dressed in Sunday suits and they were men who appear to be in their forties or older. Some appear to be much older.

W HY would any man at any time in history, past or present, voluntarily expose himself to danger and death? There are many theories. Author David Weddle, writing about the life of film director Sam Peckinpah, discusses "how at the very edge of death one feels life most keenly, even with a strange elation." As the encierro can bring one to the very edge of death, perhaps this is it.

Maybe, as famous bullrunner Matt Carney once said, "The only reason to run with bulls is just for the lark of it."

One who knows the encierro well and understands the incredible beauty of it is veteran Scottish runner Angus MacSwan. My first sighting of MacSwan in Fiesta was in the encierro. I first saw Angus running "on the horns" and a moment later he was part of the herd, surrounded by Miura bulls, racing up the center of Estafeta.

MacSwan describes running bulls and the reason for running this way, "If it is about bravery at all, the trick about being brave is not being too brave. If it is about ability at all, it is much more about luck. You run with the bulls for the feeling, because ... if you can just get it all to come right, then for a few moments you feel as if you're flying on the ground and kissing the sky."

A very different view was provided by a British-born beauty, a woman named Jackie who worked as a journalist in Saudi Arabia and traveled to Fiesta every year. She once asked, "How dead must a person be inside to have a need to come so close to death in order to feel alive?"

It is likely the first mozos ran for the alegría, the sheer joy of it. In older times, both life and Fiesta were more primitive and the days of dancing were but a brief respite from arduous and laborious lives. The release of energy and eruption of emotion in those early Fiestas must have been a powerful source of adrenalin. Perhaps the first runners were cognizant of what a privilege it is to participate in the early morning encierro, pacing a herd of fighting bulls as they run toward their destiny, a brave and noble death in the afternoon.

There was always great danger in the running and with each year the danger has escalated. The heightened danger has nothing to do with the bulls. The risks have grown as more and more runners

crowd these narrow streets. The earliest photographs of Fiesta show very few men in the encierro, only a handful. Their number has grown to the point where there will be thousands of runners in the street this first morning of this *feria*. Whatever the motivation of the first runners years ago, today there are complex motivations driving some men to run with the bulls – reasons other than joy. Modern machismo and the vanity of some men, stimulated by television and press coverage, has probably significantly changed the character of the encierro.

The city will be fully awake soon. Those who are not yet awake will be roused by stirring *dianas*, the morning music of Fiesta. The official band of the Fiesta is a formally attired marching unit, *La Pamplonesa*, and they are charged with the responsibility of waking the city each morning for the bullrun. After hearing three or four recognizable notes from a flute-like instrument called a *txistu*, sleeping revelers rise from the dead, struggle to their feet, stumble, knock over chairs, and hurry to join the throng forming behind the band. They travel the whole city with the band, dancing with hands above their heads, twirling and leaping. All along the route, exhausted people awaken from sleep in parks and abandon friends in cafés. Beautiful women and handsome men break from their embrace to join in as the band parades through Plaza del Castillo. It is an amazing sight and a scene that plays out every morning. All this begins just after dawn and leads up to the running of the bulls. With hands held high over their heads and feet tapping the beat, dancers turn, twist, twirl and charge down the street after the band.

This is how days begin in Pamplona and how days end in Pamplona, with music. Whatever hours you choose to rest, day or night, the scene outside your door never changes much. There is always music. In fact the whole cycle of life in Fiesta is like a classical symphony, marked by major and minor movements, with the music being orchestrated by the city fathers, the organizers of the bullfights and the leaders of *las peñas*, local Fiesta organiza-

OPPOSITE PAGE: *Standing room only in the street and on the balconies above Estafeta moments before the rocket fires.*

tions. La Pamplonesa ends its early morning round in the bullring, playing for the thousands of people who jam the plaza de toros awaiting the appearance of the bulls and runners. They paid a pittance for their seat in the bullring. But each year the arena becomes more crowded with spectators, particularly on the first few mornings.

The people lucky enough to have a seat to view the conclusion of this morning's encierro arrived at the plaza de toros a half-hour early. Those on the other end of the run, the ones who line the top of the wall alongside *Santo Domingo* to see the bulls released from the corral arrived at their positions hours before. Thousands will crowd balconies along the route and they know the encierro happens so fast that it can begin and end before you can get out on the balcony to take a look. The half-mile course with an uphill slope at the outset was until recently uneven ground of old cobblestone. The route was paved over in the nineties making the encierro even faster.

The average time span of the encierro is less than three and a half minutes, and it is often as much as a minute faster. The bulls run with the speed of thoroughbred horses at the beginning of the course. They run like lightning and sound like thunder, and throughout the course they sustain a pace no human can match in the madness of it all.

The encierro is one of the most dangerous and exhilarating rituals on earth. This is true even for spectators. The beauty of the running robs you of breath. It is a terrible beauty. Bulls and men racing together, blending in a moment in time, the animal relying on its primitive instincts in a man-made environment while man abandons the barriers that have separated him from the beasts for centuries.

The running is a thing of great grace and of awful terror, and it can alternate between those two states many times in less than two minutes. The cheers of thousands in one section of the route can be drowned out by a wail of horror from spectators in another. The bravery, whether intentional or accidental, of a runner flashing in front of the horns of a bull for a moment is as dramatic as seeing a bull suddenly swerve in a microsecond of time, gore a runner, carry him up

From shadow to sunlight the bulls and runners turn out of Plaza Consistorial into Calle Mercaderes. Horns high, the bulls push a mass of humanity in front of them toward a part of the course that will be even more crowded.

the street on his horn and shake him loose without breaking stride.

One glance expands the emotions of the observer and another brings those emotions to a hard, sharp edge. Hearts sing and sink only to sing again. When it is done, runners and spectators alike are spent. Then comes a rush of euphoria replacing the exhaustion.

The last minutes before the running is a time few recall. The most solitary of individuals melt into the collective experience in the final moments before the rocket is fired signaling the start of the encierro. There is little swaggering or arrogance in the street except among the uninitiated.

THE encierro is a ritual with its form prescribed, but what might occur during the run, within that predictable form, is absolutely unpredictable. It may be a very fast and smooth encierro, bulls racing up the center of the street without molesting anyone, covering the course in near record time. Perhaps all the runners will behave nobly and bring no harm to one another. Then again, the morning could turn into a bloodbath. The encierro could last ten minutes or more, signalling disaster punctuated by the wail of sirens as ambulances carry away casualties.

This morning there will be thousands in the street who have no idea what the encierro is about, and they will be joined by six bulls unaccustomed to encountering men on foot. The steers who run with the bulls every day year after year in the street return and are accustomed to the route, though in recent years the steers have also inflicted injuries on runners. Experienced runners understand the risks well and their expressions are serious as they count down the seconds to the rocket. In these final moments before the encierro, a raw, nervous energy is transmitted from the bulls themselves.

The animals sense something out of the ordinary is about to occur. Last night was the last night of their lives. They will be killed this afternoon in the bullring. They obviously cannot sense their impending death, but they have spent a restless night in strange sur-roundings far different from the quiet, peaceful range they roamed for four years and the secluded corral they shared for a few days across the river. Late last night they were moved to this stone and wood corral off Santo Domingo, and all night they heard chatter, music and singing in the streets near them.

The bulls also noticed the early morning movement and pres-ence of *pastores*, experienced bull herders who will be posted along the whole course of the run. The pastores, men who save lives every year, are identified by long sticks in their hands as they casually make their way to their positions. Similarly, the man who will light the rocket signaling the release of the bulls also strolls the street, carrying the rockets and walking in the opposite direction down Santo Domingo, toward the corral.

In the midst of all this unusual activity, the bulls see the move-ment of the steers in their corral and sense they are about to be released. The energy field emanating from the unseen bulls behind the stone and wooden walls infects the runners in the street and is transmitted to the spectators lining the route; those crowded on balconies and others balancing and roosting wherever space is available.

If the bulls break out of the corral together they should run well, for their predisposition to stay together in a herd is greater than their instinct to attack. If they are separated, the bull that is alone will attack.

In the closing moments before the rocket, runners' stomachs tighten, mouths go more dry, lips stick and limbs tremble in anticipation of the explosion of danger and death in the form of six bulls. As humans pace uneasily in the street, the bulls move restlessly in the corral. The bulls cannot be seen by the runners, only sensed. Though blocked from the view of all, the presence of the bulls is so formidable that it is forcefully felt. It is as if their aura is advancing ahead of them, permeating all of Pamplona.

When the gate swings open, the bulls often walk a few paces out of the corral, a sight unnerving in its confidence. Sometimes the bulls trot the first few steps. Then, in one step, they gallop into high gear and attain a speed no human can match but for a short distance.

THE encierro course is laid out over narrow streets and is bounded by old balconied buildings and wooden barricades blocking off cross streets and plazas and defining the course as it crosses Plaza Consistorial and an intersection known as *Teléfonos*. Behind the barricades are medics, ambulance drivers, policemen and photographers. The bulls are accompanied by steers and oxen, animals trained to herd bulls. All of their lives these bulls have been led to water, food and new pastures by oxen and steers and their training is to obediently follow them. The steers and oxen in Pamplona run year after year and know the route well. The bulls, never having run the course or encountered man on foot, are confused, and rely on the steers to lead them.

Ideally, all of the animals should swiftly complete the course in an organized fashion, flying down the street in formation, shoulder to shoulder. But things can go wrong, giving way to injuries, creating chaos in the street, and escalating the obvious danger to serious injuries and sometimes death.

Thousands are in the street, spread from the corral to the bull-ring as the first rocket sounds. Most are men. A few are women, mostly tourists. Of the thousands in the street, only a few hundred have any real understanding of what is now happening and will actually attempt to run with the bulls. The others, the bulk of the crowd, are extremely inexperienced – tourists and first-timers who pose a danger to themselves and others. It is this group which is at the greatest risk of injury and death according to hospital statistics.

There have been horrifying injuries inflicted on first-timers in the last few years and in 1995 a handsome young American runner was gored to death in front of the town hall less than thirty seconds into his first encierro experience.

Each year more people step into the street ignorant of the rules of the run, and knowing nothing about the approach one should take in the encierro. But it is not always the inexperienced who suffer injuries. Some of the most experienced and talented bullrunners go down as well and sustain severe injuries. There have been deaths in the street along the course and in the bullring itself. As the streets grow more crowded each year, it is inevitable that the growing horde will continue to cause problems for bulls and runners alike, including mountainous pileups of fallen runners in the street, causing more injuries and more deaths.

As crowded as the streets are, there is always space around the bulls and especially in front of the horns. This space is referred to by experienced runners as the "aura of danger" and only a small number of mozos will run within the aura of danger. In an instant the great runners glide gracefully into the aura of danger and run on the horns. In this moment a runner's love of the experience conquers his fear of it. It is said that when a man moves alongside or into the pack and is accepted by the herd, in that instant of time, transcendence occurs. To run in close, within the aura of danger, you must consciously overcome all natural instincts of self-preservation and

The sun shines in two spots on the encierro route, the place in the background of this photograph where Mercaderes begins and the entrance to the bullring. This picture taken by Joanna Pinneo from a barricade on the route captures the gracefulness of the encierro at one of the most dangerous points.

force yourself into the center of the street, that place where death and destiny dance at the speed of light.

WHEN a bull has become separated from the herd one may hear shouts of *suelto*, the term for a lone bull. A bull may become separated from the herd through no fault of its own by slipping down and being left behind, or maybe it separates because it is a maverick. Either way, the result will be the same. This lost bull's instinct will be to define his terrain and attack anything that moves within that territory. It is the suelto that will most likely injure, maim, gore and kill. And it is only skilled pastores and the most experienced and brave runners who can lure a suelto back onto the course and into the bullring. On an infamous bloody day in the late eighties all six bulls ended up separated from one another and consequently there were terrible injuries.

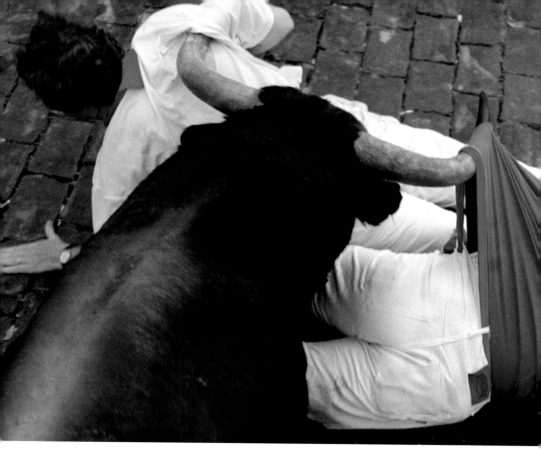

This photograph taken by Desmond Boylan was awarded the Concurso Periodístico Internacional San Fermín in Pamplona. It depicts something even the most experienced runner would find hard to believe: a bull hooks two runners, one on each horn.

A bull that breaks from the corral first and has no contact with the herd can be as dangerous as one left behind. A bad goring occurred in Santo Domingo in 1993 when a bull led the pack, swerved and gored a local runner just seconds into the encierro. Out front and alone, this thirteen hundred pound bull from the Pedro Romero Ranch, "*Papelero*," attacked almost immediately. If the steers had broken first from the corral this may not have happened. In this instance, Papelero's horn ripped into the runner's body, removing a fifteen centimeter chunk of skin from his upper buttocks before becoming hooked in the runner's sash. For this reason most runners do not wear belts, and they tie their sashes and pañuelos in slipknots.

After hooking the runner on his horn, Papelero dragged him

forty meters up Santo Domingo with the runner's head bouncing and hitting the stone street along the way.

This injury is not the worst injury sustained in recent years. It was graded grave by physicians, but it was minor in comparison to many other gorings. What makes this incident particularly note-worthy is what it illustrates about the type of bull one encounters in the encierro. Even after swerving, goring and hooking the mozo, Papelero remained in the lead, still setting the pace for the herd in an awesome demonstration of speed and strength, carrying the run-ner uphill on his horn.

THERE are many things people should know before running the bulls, and there are probably at least as many theories about running as there are runners. These theories are recounted at bars on Plaza

There is serious danger in this innocent-looking scene. Near the entrance to the bullring a suelto or solo bull is separated from the herd, turned in the wrong direction, stalled out. The bull has chosen not to follow the steer in the top of the frame, and the street has all but cleared out. Only a few experienced runners work to attract the bull and run it into the bullring.

del Castillo every morning following the run and most experienced runners welcome the opportunity to chat with novices about the complexities of the encierro. Though the route of the run has not changed much in the last century and a half, the character of the encierro has definitely changed. With live television coverage, instant replays, delayed worldwide broadcasts and exhaustive local newspaper coverage, sometimes the spectacle can seem more a running of the men than a running of the bulls. At the outdoor cafés on the plaza immediately after the encierro, the conversation among many runners is talk about themselves, with little mention of the bulls in whose honor the encierro exists. There is no way of turning back the clock to the time before commercial photo shops sold encierro prints immediately after the run and computer generated images were available allowing anyone to carry home a digitally manipulated photo that purports to show them in the encierro though they slept through it. Vanity is an enemy of the spirit of the event, but only a nuisance, for nothing can change the nature of the thing.

There are some runners who understand the history and tradition, men who hold a deep respect for the bulls. These men consider it an honor to stride a few steps with the bulls in the early morning air. They comprehend the purpose of Fiesta, and they honor the rules of the encierro, which are few.

The most important published regulation states that it is expressly forbidden to call to the bulls, attract them in any way, touch them, hold on to any part of them, or otherwise do anything which may distract them or impede their journey to the ring. It is extremely dangerous to attract or touch a bull and seldom is the runner who acts to alter the bull's course the one who is injured. Often an innocent runner is hit as the bull swerves or turns after being touched, slapped, hit or having its tail pulled. Some young foreigners, caught up in the rodeo imagery of their own culture, having no understanding of this breed of bull or of the encierro, are often the rule breakers and their actions are more a matter of brash ignorance than malicious intent.

During the encierro, runners' pulse rates have been recorded

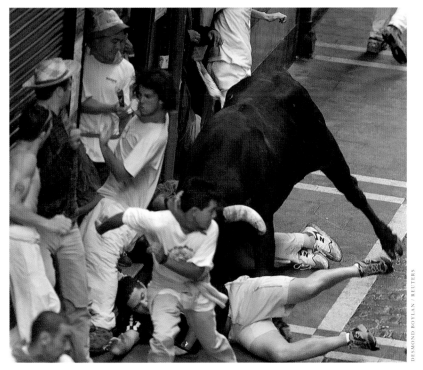

A solo bull or suelto, separated from the herd, begins to rampage. One runner correctly attempts to lure the bull toward the plaza de toros; several bystanders appear as oblivious to the danger as they were when they lost count of the drinks they consumed during the night.

soaring to way more than twice their normal rates, and with so much adrenalin in their systems, it is easy to understand some of the erratic and dangerous actions of newcomers to the running. Lest one should think he can disregard the rule about touching an animal or attracting a bull's attention, he should know the rule is sometimes enforced promptly and unofficially by local runners who pummel the violator immediately after the encierro. In one way or another, this rule is usually enforced.

On the other hand, some rules of the encierro, like the one which banned women from the run for many years, I've never seen enforced, and I'm not certain it exists any longer. Also, the rule that specifies that participants be at least eighteen and not drunk or drugged is rarely enforced. And given the outlandish attire in Fiesta,

CORRALILLO

Arga

SANTO DOMINGO

ENCIERRO
COURSE

PLAZA
CONSISTORIAL

MERCADERES

LA CURVA

ESTAFETA

PLAZA DEL
CASTILLO

TELEFONOS

CALLEJÓN

PLAZA DE TOROS

I used to wonder where the police drew the line on the rule stating that runners must be properly dressed. That question was answered when a nude Brit attempted to "streak" the bulls a few years back and was yanked out of the street by the police and taken to jail.

In addition to the rules of the run, one should know some other things about the encierro before getting into the street. First, one should know that the course essentially has seven sections.

The first five sections are streets or plazas; Santo Domingo, Plaza Consistorial, Mercaderes, Estafeta and Teléfonos. Finally there is the tunnel-like narrow passageway leading into the bullring, the *callejón*, and then the bullring itself. Each section is different from the others and requires a separate strategy drawn to the particular challenges presented by that part of the course. You can learn a lot about these things in conversation with experienced runners who ordinarily will generously share information. Most will first give you the best advice a newcomer can receive by telling you to stay out of the street altogether.

The first section is a stone canyon called Santo Domingo. It is a steep uphill stretch, hardly wide enough to allow the animals to squeeze through, much less accommodate men. Here the bulls will be fastest as they are fresh and running uphill. On an uphill grade they run full out, whereas on a downward slope, like the slight downhill grade at the entrance to the ring, the bulls are more careful about their footing. In Santo Domingo they cover the first hundred meters almost as fast as an Olympic sprinter. This, the bottom of the course, is usually populated by a few experienced runners, mostly Navarrans. No first-timer should consider running here.

Then there is the passage through Plaza Consistorial in front of the town hall, which covers level ground. It is a wider section, but the forgiving appearance of this terrain masks its treacherous nature which only reveals itself at the moment hundreds of runners are flushed out of the tight confines of Santo Domingo and into this plaza.

As the course twists out of town hall plaza onto a short street called Mercaderes, both bulls and men are bathed in and blinded by bright sunlight. This flash of light can disorient those who are not expecting it. Mercaderes is a short street connecting to Estafeta and it is not a street on which any newcomer belongs under any circumstances for there is an infamous 90-degree turn at its end, *la curva*, a dangerous trap for the unknowing.

The longest, straightest, most crowded part of the run is Estafeta. Estafeta leads to a densely packed area known as Teléfonos and finally those in Teléfonos, the top of the run, are funneled into the bullring. Because of the early hour, the position of the sun, and the tall buildings lining the route, most of the encierro is in shadow. But when the bulls and runners turn onto Mercaderes and later step onto the sand floor of the bullring, rays of sunlight showcase them.

The worst injuries have occurred at the bottom and at the top of the run, on Santo Domingo and in the callejón. However, the two most dangerous parts of the encierro are probably the curve into Estafeta and the bullring itself where there have been several deaths.

"There is no way to run with bulls," laments a veteran Navarran runner, a lifelong resident of Pamplona and an acknowledged maestro of Estafeta. As a younger man he used to race the full length of Estafeta on the horns. Now he no longer runs. He gave it up years ago because of the crowds and the large number of steers and oxen. He says it is impossible to get through the people to be near the animals and if one is lucky enough to get in close to an animal it is as likely to be a steer as a bull, and the danger is the runners, not the bulls.

Like many old timers, he longs for the days of clean streets, a time when there were fewer runners and a runner could get a better view of the approaching herd and run close in. He laughs and says of the mayor of Pamplona, "The mayor lays awake at night worrying over a headline around the world saying 'Ten Foreigners Killed By Bulls,'" the kind of publicity which would hurt the Fiesta's popularity and decrease the money it brings to the city each year. He believes that if the mayor could tie a protective guard, a rubber blanket, around the bulls or remove the horns for three minutes every morning, that would be done.

Among serious runners the complaint about crowded conditions is a common one. Many runners swear each year will be their last because of the crowds. Of those who do not run in the encierro at all, just as many swear each Fiesta is their last because of the high prices. Nonetheless, all of them return, resigned that there will never be a rollback in either the prices or in the size of the crowd in the encierro.

THIS morning the streets will be so crowded in some sections that the runners will not even be able to see the bulls approaching. The noise of the crowd will be so loud that they will not hear hooves pounding on the street. It is an unnerving experience for novices and you cannot just stand in the street and wait for the bulls, because you will be flattened by panicked runners.

Running the bulls was always a difficult thing to do under any circumstances and it is now an almost impossible thing to do well under present circumstances. The better runners compensate for crowded conditions in many ways and some are very good at it.

The police will only allow you to enter the route in the portion that comprises the first part or lower end of the course – the area between the town hall plaza and the corrals on Santo Domingo. Police will not allow any entry anywhere after 7:30 a.m. On some mornings, especially weekends, the act of working one's way through the crowds and crawling between the crossbars of the barricades to enter the course is an exhausting experience.

Police lines normally hold all runners in the bottom of the course until about four or five minutes before the rocket. Then the runners are allowed to advance to a point just beyond the halfway mark where they encounter a second police line that will hold them a few more minutes. When the runners are released from the second police line, they spread along the entire length of the course.

When the last police line moves, allowing runners to advance, some sprint up the street toward the ring. Others calmly stroll to the section of the street they will run. Experienced runners know their turf well. And they know what happens when the first rocket explodes.

On the first rocket hundreds race into the bullring minutes ahead of any danger. The locals jokingly call these guys *valientes*, the valiant ones. Occasionally one of the local papers will memorialize the moment when the first frightened runner races into the bullring a full two minutes ahead of the first bull, placing the valiente's image on the front page. Spaniards, and the people of Pamplona in particular, are famous for making light of even the most serious things.

Bulls and steers run in Estafeta as the crowd moves clear of the space nearest the horns and around the herd.

As the remaining seconds to the rocket are counted down, the street is set like a stage poised for combat. During the encierro the street feels like war. The same emotions and instincts are present. It is in a true sense a primal, savage ritual. There are no human controls. The sound, smell and horror of it all unfolds without any boundaries except the barricades which only contain the flow and insure that no one in the street shall be detoured from their appointment with the brute force of the bulls.

In the midst of madness, in the center of the street, great runners are portraits of composure. While most feel as if fear is scraping their very soul, other's hearts swell with happiness. Some cling to walls and fight off instincts to use fellow humans as shields, regressing into their deepest survival instincts, the place within all of us where cowardice lies. While many frantically drown beneath the terror of it, great Navarran runners sail on the surface of it, running the center of the street, often with a bull's horn near their heart.

As CHURCH bells ring in the distance and the rocket shoots skyward with a whooshing sound, Pamplona is paralyzed. Everything stops. While the rocket is breaking up into white wisps trailing against the morning sky, there is an eerie silence. Then the gate to the corral swings open. No one hears its sound. When the bulls move into the street almost no one hears their hooves striking pavement.

Those in the street awaiting the bulls can make no noise. Their throats are too tight to speak, their mouths too dry to form words. Fear can be seen on their frozen faces. Runners feel a dread-tinged anticipation that can only be washed away by cold adrenalin.

The silence is broken by the soft sound of rubber-soled running shoes shuffling over pavement and cobblestones as runners nervously begin to advance, then the crowd noise begins to swell. Once the street is flushed of the valientes, the front runners, the real problems begin. Overcrowding grows as the bulls push the mass of humans up the tight corridors comprising the course. The narrow passages which make up the route cannot contain the mob and there is nowhere for them to go except up the street toward the bullring, against the wall where many are already plastered to the stone, or face down in the street.

A few longtime runners have spotters, friends signaling them from balconies, using hand signals to let them know whether the herd is bunched together or strung out, being led by steers or bulls, favoring one side of the street or the other. Based on these signals and his trust of the person on the balcony, the runner will break for a position in the street calculated to place him near the bulls when they arrive. This system is good strategy, but it relies on the expertise of the observer and the bond of confidence between partners, not solely on the responses of the runner.

Many runners employ a tactic that came into fashion in the modern era. They stand on the edge of the street or in a doorway and keep looking down the street after the rocket fires, looking for the first horn. They pay close attention to the movement and facial expressions of runners coming toward them. The closer the herd to the runners, the harder the runners' arms pump, the more frantic their expressions become. The people come in waves, and the last wave before the horns is always out of control.

Some athletic runners stand near the center of the street, bobbing and weaving around the crush of oncoming runners as they await the herd. A more classic and old fashioned technique, perhaps the best one, is still practiced by some Navarrans. It dates back to earlier days when the streets were less crowded. These runners start running on the rocket, moving toward their position in the middle of the street. They know that at the moment of truth there will be nothing in the center of the street but bulls. When the bulls arrive, they pick them up and take the herd as far as they can before they are outrun, fall or find themselves pushed out of the flow.

When the bulls are near, experienced runners break and run in one of several different styles. The most common way of running is a style that could be called lane running, practiced by people who consistently run in the same imaginary trace. Most lane runners prefer an outside path next to a barricade which can be an emergency exit of sorts. They know if they must get out of the run for any reason, the best way out is going underneath a fence. There is never time to climb over and that kind of movement can attract a bull and cause the runner to become impaled on the horn against the fence. Runners going under the barricade, diving out of the street are quickly pulled to safety by police and medics. For this reason alone, many run lanes.

Those few extraordinary runners who still break for and hold the center of the street know it is the place where there are always bulls, and there is no way out for them in the event of an emergency. But these experienced runners know what to do if they should fall or get pushed down in the bulls' path. When you are laid out on the street, helpless in front of charging bulls, you should do nothing, nothing at all. If downed in the encierro, cover your head and remain motionless until someone offers you aid or you hear the third and final rocket signifying the run is over.

Many a runner has had a whole herd hurdle over him as he lay in the street, escaping unscathed. A *toro bravo* is sure-

Red, white and black. A runner in the center of the street, in the aura of danger, moves into position to run "on the horns."

footed and runs with his eyes cast downward. Though they do not see all that well, they see best where they eat, at ground level. They will not intentionally place a hoof on something that appears as uneven terrain which could cause them to stumble and lose their footing.

Exceptional runners are true artists. If you trace the lines of a still photograph depicting an artistic runner with a bull, the outline of both animal and man will be fluid and graceful. The greatest beauty in an encierro is to see an artistic runner on the horns of a bull, a brave bull fearlessly racing wide open through the streets toward an unknown destination and a man who has abandoned all caution to run close in. These artists accept their fate on any given morning. In their vernacular, they "take whatever the Saint gives them," knowing some encierros will be better than others.

Other men are dominating runners, men who seem to be challenging the bull for its space in the street, battling other bullrunners as they fight for the horn. Among these men are great runners of sueltos, men who can attract, turn, control and lure a solo bull to the plaza and corrals.

Some matadors have run the encierro, while others in the field refuse to go near it. An ongoing controversy continues about

SANTIAGO LYON / ASSOCIATED PRESS

A downed runner has a 1,200 pound bull fall on him. The impact causes the runner's watch to fly free.

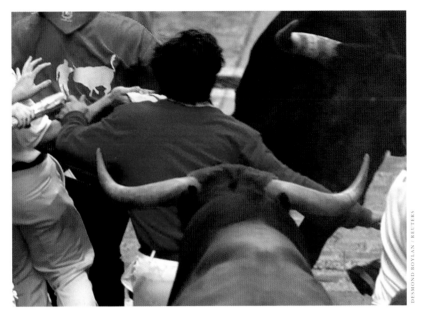

On the horns of a dilemma. Sandwiched between two bulls running in opposite directions, the runner in blue is saved by the movement of another runner that attracts the black bull.

whether the morning sprint through the streets diminishes or enhances the bulls' performance when they face the matadors in the afternoon corrida. Many believe the run is of benefit; however, it seems every year at least one bull is injured in the encierro and disqualified for the afternoon bullfight, requiring a substitution. One of the best bull breeders in Spain, a man who raises bulls that Pamplona would love to have for a corrida, refuses to bring his bulls to Fiesta because he feels the encierro is an insult to the great *casta* or breeding of his bulls.

Some of the finest Navarran bullrunners have actually fought young bulls and *vacas*, wild cows, as amateurs, and others have worked as ranch hands on *fincas* where toros bravos are raised. These men understand the behavior of bulls and approach the encierro with a level of knowledge and experience far beyond that of the ordinary summer runner. Occasionally something will occur in an encierro between a runner and a bull which makes the runner's expertise evident to all observers.

The temptation to list names of brave, talented, brilliant and inspirational Navarran runners and recount some of their legendary encierro exploits is hard to resist. However, to omit their names and accomplishments is to honor them, for the Navarrans frown upon anyone bringing attention to himself or another as a bullrunner. Their feeling is that this most public spectacle is a very private affair. To them it matters not whether one runs valiente, in an outside lane, in a dominating or even an artistic way. It matters not whether one runs nobly or disgracefully, bravely or cowardly, or even whether one runs at all. They care about how they run and their goal is to run noble y bravo.

As spectacular as the encierro is, to place the event in perspective one must realize that each of the eight encierros last about three minutes and the total time devoted to bullrunning during the week is less than a half hour total, while the Fiesta itself, from opening to closing, spans nine days and nights.

The unspoken code is that one who feels joy or what the Spanish call alegría, and is led to run "just for the lark of it" should not run to bring attention to himself, to be heroic, or to prove anything to himself or others. In this excessively public phenomenon, one's experience is largely private.

THIS morning I entered the course an hour early at town hall and wandered down to a small street behind the market and off Santo Domingo. A lot of people trekked through the little street this morning. It's a tradition left over from a time when a popular bar and billet stood here, *Casa Marceliano*, a place favored by Ernest Hemingway. There is another bar along this street today and a news stand as well. Some runners had coffee and several had *caldo*, an oily broth which warms the body in chilly weather. Most purchased a daily newspaper from the news stand next to the bar. They rolled the paper to carry in the encierro. Superstitious fellows buy the same paper every day. Most carry a local Pamplona paper. One American runs with a copy of *The Wall Street Journal*. The newspaper is seldom used by anyone in the encierro, though an experienced

Adorned with the shirt of a runner, a bull negotiates the portion of the run known as Teléfonos.

runner might use the paper baton to attract the attention of a suelto. Others might imagine themselves unfurling the newspaper to
use it like a matador would, a highly improbable scenario.

Each day pictures of the six bulls and their listed weights are in
all of the daily papers and this morning most runners reviewed the
photos, noting the color and patterns of their hides. One of the most
important things a runner should do in the street is count the bulls as
they pass you. This counting of bulls is something newcomers have
trouble mastering, but the importance of knowing at all times how
many bulls are still charging up the street behind you is obvious.

The bulls are strung out as they near the callejón or tunnel leading into the bullring. This wide, downhill portion of the run is framed by tall trees, giving it a different feel from the rest of the route.

MELONY BARRIOS MOULTON

Before the encierro some runners attempt to distract themselves from their nervousness by reading reviews of the previous day's bullfight or news stories. This morning there was good-natured kidding among a group of old friends gathered in the street, a private joke they shared. Often there are light moments in this side street before the run. The ambiance is something like a locker room before a big game. All are aware that a close friend standing near could be gravely wounded or killed in the next few minutes. No one speaks of these things and few even allude to the encierro which is now minutes away.

This morning people passed this anxious time in various ways. Some were solitary, drifting up a high hill at the end of the street. There they stretched, limbering their bodies and loosening their nerves. One of the loners stood for a long time staring out toward the Pyrenees. Others stayed in the street and were sociable. As the time neared everyone traded hearty hugs, wishing each other *suerte,* or luck. There was music this morning, a small troupe playing wind instruments accompanied by a little drum.

As we walked from the former Marceliano's into Santo Domingo to pray at the statue of the Saint, everything about the morning turned a bit more solemn. In the distance we could hear the faint sound of a brass band. Strains of one of the morning anthems drifted along crooked streets, echoed off tall walls and reached us as a suggestion of a song, a musical murmur.

Those who have run for years know the danger best and probably feel far more fear than rookies. The area in the street around the statue in the niche was crowded with veteran runners making the sign of the cross and praying for five minutes of grace. As the song to the Saint began, my friends moved up the street to the places where they would run. I nervously paced as the runners sang their prayer.

The singing stopped in Santo Domingo, the rocket fired and I ran a few short steps in the left outside lane, then looked back over my shoulder and saw a scene developing that could end only one way. A friend was moving into perfect position. I ran up against the wall, stopped and watched him run on the right horn of the lead bull, move to the side in one quick step to let it pass, then pick up the second bull and run on the horns once more. It was a spectacular sight and I remained thrilled long afterwards.

In Santo Domingo the run is a few seconds at most, though it seems to last much longer sometimes. This morning the herd was tightly packed, running well. None of the bulls were even looking, much less hooking. Judging by the quick final rocket at the bullring and the absence of sirens, it seems it was fast and relatively safe all the way.

I watched the last oxen bound up the street, the clean-up *cabestros*, monstrous bovines that are released late each morning and used by the pastores to help herd any strays or sueltos when necessary. As the last rocket sounded, announcing the end of the encierro, the door of a bar on Santo Domingo opened. I ducked in with friends, grabbing a coffee from the bar. The day had started well as I saw a great friend have a dramatic moment on the horns and popped into a Pamplona bar for coffee, all in less than five minutes. One of our Spanish friends who is often bleeding, stitched, beat up or bandaged from a run-in with the horns joined us for coffee. Today all he got from the medics wearing the blue sweaters with red crosses was hugs. He ran unscathed. Everyone in our group came out in great shape today.

A number of old Santo Domingo hands approached our friend in the bar with congratulations and slaps on the back for the graceful full-speed ballet he performed in the tight tracks of Santo Domingo. The recipient of the praise accepted the compliments with grace. No one said much else about the encierro as we became absorbed in a gambling game to determine who would pay for the round of drinks.

With our coffees finished and paid for by the loser of the game, we strolled up the hill to Plaza del Castillo and joined a large contingent of runners at *Bar Txoko*. Txoko is a Basque word that simply means "corner" and is pronounced "choko." Some of the extraordinary local runners are always there, and for years many foreigners have drifted to this place after the encierro. Some of those at Bar

Txoko have been there all morning and all night. Each morning these characters listen to the encierro. They glance at their wristwatch when the first rocket is fired and then count the seconds until the next rocket is heard. The first boom only indicates the opening of the gate. The second rocket signals that the sixth and last bull has left the corral. The split between these two rockets can tell one a great deal. A long lapse of time indicates that one or more bulls lagged behind in the corral, that there is not a tight pack and the bulls may be strung out, possibly in multiple groups, and there may be stragglers or sueltos for runners to contend with. As a caveat, one should also understand that the rockets are lighted with a cigarette lighter and have long wicks, thus, even when the herd flies through the gate shoulder to shoulder, there may be as much as 16 to 20 seconds between the first two rockets. If a starter pistol were used in this circumstance, it would often sound back to back shots. This morning when those in the cafés heard the third and final rocket less than three minutes from the first, they clinked

Herding tightly, running the way a herd should under ideal conditions, the horns push the crowd up the street.

glasses in a toast to the Saint. Some mornings they hear ambulance sirens. Today there were none.

Some stay at Bar Txoko for a long while after the run. Others drift down the way to other cafés around the plaza, but the bullring remains crowded with spectators and runners for a long time after the final rocket fires at the end of the encierro. Many who run the last leg of the course into the bullring remain there after the bulls have been caped into the corrals. These guys play with the wild cows that are released into the ring after the bulls are locked away. It's great fun but it can be dangerous. A few of my friends still play with the vacas, though most drink at Txoko and exchange accounts of their encierro experience. After a couple of drinks, many groups amble off in search of breakfast.

The sun seems suddenly bright following the encierro. Some mornings the sky is filled with multi-colored hot air balloons that lazily float above Fiesta against a crisp blue sky. Once a helicopter hovered over the run, probably a documentary camera crew. The noise was so great that the runners below did not hear the first two rockets. It was the last time any kind of aircraft was granted permission to fly over the encierro. Even the hot air balloons do not appear until 8:15 a.m., well after the last rocket is usually fired. With the encierro finished for 24 hours, Fiesta moves from a state of frenzied excitement to a quiet calm.

EDWARD GANS

Geronimo, a local Basque, ran with the bulls in Pamplona way over fifty years. He carried old photographs with him from his early runs. He was seriously injured on occasion and often said he expected to die on the horns. That did not happen.

One of the balloons cast a shadow on part of the plaza today and a few people tried to walk in the shade of its shadow. During the hot days of Fiesta

A sea of red berets in Irun, a town near Pamplona that celebrates a continuous 24-hour fiesta a week before Sanfermines. All of northern Spain is alive with fiestas in summer; most require phenomenal endurance.

one walks across the city carefully, trying always to stay in the shade. After an all-nighter, when the sun sets up shop on top of the town, some seek shade with the vigor of a vampire.

THE running of the bulls takes but minutes. Another principal activity in Pamplona, one that fills much of the remaining 23.9 hours a day, is the *running of the bars*.

The town has more bars than Bangkok. Some of the drinks have exotic names and equally unusual ingredients: *kalimotxo, Kaiku y cognac, shampú, revuelto, manzanilla, carajillo de cognac, fino, caldo, clarete*, and *pacharán*, which the Basques spell *patxaran*. There is also a Basque cider known by several names, as well as the more familiar sangria, Cuba libre, bloody marys, gin, vodka, and some bottles of scotch with suspicious names like McGintys that no one has heard of, and, of course there is enough low-grade wine and beer to fill an ocean. There are various brands of bottled beer and some drafts that come in giant two-handed containers.

JOANNA B. PINNEO / AURORA & QUANTA PRODUCTIONS

Squirting a stream from a glass container, this Navarran exhibits expertise.

The drink in the morning following the encierro is Kaiku y cognac, a concoction that combines a sweet bottle of a thick chocolate or vanilla drink, the kind of stuff a little kid would drink, poured into a glass half filled with a low-grade, fiery cognac, served straight up or over rocks. As the Spanish do not normally use nearly as much ice as Americans do, the rock pile is often low at this hour. Like everything, Kaiku y cognac is a matter of taste. Some love the drink. Others find it ghastly, especially considering the early hour.

Young Basques invented their own drink, kalimotxo, which was first spotted in the peña bars in the seventies; the drink is an amazing combination of sugar, caffeine and alcohol which has to be served over ice to be tolerable. Kalimotxo is a 50/50 mix of cheap red wine and Coca-Cola. Purists, if the word can even be used tongue in cheek here, advise that using either a good wine or another brand of soft drink destroys the integrity of the libation. For years the drink was served by a barkeep first pouring a half glass of wine from a jug and then dumping coke out of a bottle to bring it to the brim. Today the drink is so popular that fountain dispensers are used; coke from one cylinder, wine from the other. Though no wine connoisseur would let a kalimotxo pass his or her lips, it is generally regarded by the masses as the "survival drink" of Fiesta based on the belief that the body will accept kalimotxo long after it has started rebelling against or rejecting mainstream drinks.

This is as good a place as any to mention a caveat about the glasses in Pamplona. In many places glasses are washed by hand, usually in warm or tepid water, and there is no way to keep them germ free due to the volume of customers at this time of year. There's not enough hot water in hell to wash all these glasses. A prevalent theory among foreigners is that drinking from these glasses and exposing oneself to these germs can be as dangerous as anything short of the encierro, so many insist their drinks be served in plastic cups.

The bars are literally door to door for blocks on some streets and there is no street in the old quarter without its share. When you see the bars in this town during the day, a time when they are not at capacity, you are struck by how uninspiring they look; long, narrow rooms with not much going for them. It may not occur to a newcomer that the rest of the year these bars actually have furniture, accessories, plants, and a particular ambiance that sets them apart from their competitors. During these weeks in July, the majority of the bars are identical in appearance, stripped down to the lowest common denominator, serving as many people as possible as quickly as possible. The bar staffs are focused, always pouring two drinks at once. A seasoned floor trader at the New York stock exchange could not handle the chaotic work of a barman in Pamplona, not to mention the hours.

There is no etiquette in the bars. If you've been standing quietly before a bartender for ten minutes, he may well serve someone else who just walks up and yells his order. Just because you are standing in front of them does not necessarily mean they can see you. The bars are so crowded by nightfall that people have to dance in place, turning in a tight circle, hands above their head. The deafening music goes 24 hours, a mix of tapes and discs ranging from traditional peña music of the Fiesta to stark techno stuff more suited for a club on Ibiza.

The drinks can be discovered by a newcomer randomly sampling them but one that should not be missed is the one they call shampú, or *champagne-limon*, a lemon sorbet soaked in good champagne. It is served in a number of places but is best in the back bar of the *Hotel Yoldi* after the bullfight.

There is a long run of bars in a narrow, twisting street called *Jarrauta* that some call "the street of broken dreams" where it is sporting to attempt to have one drink in each bar on the north side of the street and then repeat the process on the south side. No one in history has made it halfway up the first side of the street.

Spanish drinking is tidal. A bar packed to the ceiling one moment can be empty five minutes later as the Spaniards have finished their one regulation drink and moved up the street. Anglos still stranded in the empty bar, having their third drink, give a sigh of relief to have so much space around them, and then another wave hits.

One reason Pamplona has so many bars is Spanish drinking customs. Even out of Fiesta, in calmer times when the bars are better appointed, a Spaniard will usually have only one drink in any given bar and then move on to another, whereas our habit is to stake out a bar and make claim to it for the evening. And a Basque's way of drinking is directly opposite that of most Anglos. The English drink their beer in pints and their spirits or hard liquor in thimblefuls. The Basques order beer in thimblefuls and their whiskey, brandy and patxaran in measures that would floor the hardiest Anglo drinker.

Going into your favorite Fiesta bar out of season can be shocking, almost traumatic. You are sure there has been a change of management for the place will exude a genteel quality, have real furniture, muted music, and customers talking quietly who appear boring. And you will notice there are pictures on the wall, and also that there is no sawdust on the floor.

Arguably the best drink in Fiesta is *agua del grifo*, water from the tap. Being mountainous country and a city set on top of stone, the water in Pamplona is probably the best you will taste anywhere. It is so rich in minerals that the locals do not drink it, for over many years it will blacken one's teeth. But there is nothing better than this drink, especially if one is lucky enough to have a bar or restaurant specializing in that rare commodity, ice. It is also true that the bottled water available in Pamplona tends to have the flavor of the plastic bottle from which it is poured. Agua del grifo is the key, the real secret, to successfully running the bars of Pamplona. If one makes the run with a local, he or she will observe the local drinking two or more waters to one glass of alcohol, and mixing in an occasional *café solo* or black coffee, pacing himself like a Kentucky-bred racehorse in the Derby, making sure he will have the gas to come around the last turn on July 13 and hit the finish line in grand form on the 14th.

While most of the bars are street level, some are in cellars and others a floor up from the street. The best way to acclimate to running the bars is to begin in the Spanish way; one drink in each establishment until you happen on to places that will be your favorites. The ambiance on the main square, Plaza del Castillo, especially at night, is brilliant and reminiscent of a bygone era; however, the drinks are more expensive here than in Calles San Nicholás and Jarrauta.

Once upon a time there were quiet places to drink in Pamplona, the lobbies of the better hotels, and this still holds true for the elegant *Hotel Tres Reyes*. The *Maisonnave*, one of Pamplona's best hotels, has a beautiful bar that is a lovely spot to pass time during the off season but in Fiesta at night it rocks like the places on San Nicholás.

Contrasting dramatically with the lovely hotel bars is the row of tents that travel from fair to fair throughout Spain. Under the tents one can buy what some refer to as dual-purpose booze, sangría and red wine in bottles with screw-on caps. It is said you can either drink the bottle of wine or jug of sangria, or dump it in the tank of your rental car and run 100 kilometers on it.

One who drinks well in Fiesta says wise foreigners will arrive early in Pamplona and use some of that spare time cleverly getting to know the names of the staff in their favorite haunts, tipping discreetly but significantly. Then when anarchy breaks out they will have increased the odds of receiving faster service and maybe getting an occasional freebie.

An oddity in Pamplona is how certain drinks traditionally are drunk only at certain times. Caldo, the warm, clear broth is taken to fortify one against the early morning chill. Kaiku y cognac is drunk only on Plaza del Castillo after the encierro, often followed by a round of bloody marys at another bar. At the sorting of the bulls behind the bullring at midday, fino, sherry, is served. *Rioja* wines grace tables during lunch. After the corrida there is shampú, which is served in some places in huge brandy *ballons*. People drink patxaran, a sweet liqueur made from endrina berries, just about anytime, though it is typically served in the evening following dinner.

It's worth noting that there are many on both the Spanish and foreign side of Fiesta who do not drink alcohol at all. There are even meetings of Alcoholics Anonymous during the celebration, evidence that it is not essential to imbibe in order to live Fiesta full out. Whether one drinks alcohol or not, if he or she misses out on running the bars of Pamplona, he or she will miss out on a large part of Fiesta.

In the bars one finds old folks, young people, even the very young, all dancing and keeping a pace that would drop most athletes to the floor. As sleep is hard to come by in Pamplona because of the unending cacophony drifting up from the street to hotel windows, one may as well join in the running of the bars.

The people of Pamplona have elevated drinking to an art form. They will pick out a roving brass band and follow it through the night, dropping off here and there with the troupe for a drink, then moving on to another bar, and then another, never having to stop because the bars never close.

PAMPLONA is a city for many things but it is not a city for plans. The sooner one learns this, the easier Fiesta will be. It is one of the things you should know and there are really only a few things one must know about Fiesta in order to enjoy it as the Navarrans do.

First, you must know that you can never go to Fiesta. Fiesta must come to you. All you can do is present yourself in Plaza del Castillo, the heart of Pamplona, and wait for Fiesta to embrace you. If your heart holds a generous spirit, your energy is positive, and you are relaxed, then Fiesta will come to you and will overcome you at the same time. In the coming days you will experience every emotion embodied in the human condition.

You should also know this rule: whenever you are in doubt during Fiesta, follow the music. Whether your doubt is because you are exhausted, confused, or lost, there will always be music in the streets all night and much of the day. The marching peña bands go wherever they wish and one who is in doubt should fall in line and follow one. A parading peña band will guide you to wherever you need to go, playing music unlike any you have heard, music you first hear with your heart.

If you have allowed Fiesta to come to you, and if you have followed the music through the night, you will know you are truly in Fiesta when you join the Navarrans in dance. That moment will come in Fiesta for everyone, the moment when you cross over from being a bystander to being a participant.

Let the music be your teacher. The music will show you how to travel the neighborhoods in the night and dance dianas at dawn, and bands will bring you to the bullfight in the afternoon.

The music will bring you to what some call the river. Some talk about swimming in the stream of Fiesta, about going with the flow, the flow around you and the flow within you. Being in the river of Fiesta, in the drift, is not about doing what your head thinks you should do or doing what your body telegraphs you to do. It is about following your feelings, hearing your heart.

AFTER the morning's run everyone's intellect tells them it is way past time to sleep and they must head straight to bed. Their instincts tell them it is way past time to eat and they must immediately find food. However, if you are in the drift, swimming in the river of Fiesta, you will do neither, for something happens in every encierro. It happens to runners and spectators alike. The adrenalin rush drives out all fatigue.

As badly as you may want or need breakfast, when you leave Bar Txoko you will wander through several bars and work your way through rounds of drinks. Every other door seems to open to a bar and more than one will detour you from your mission. Somewhere along the line, between Bar Txoko and breakfast, a discussion will

A line forms early in the morning for the oldest churro factory in the world. Located in the narrow lane leading to the market, the factory's ovens rest against Roman walls. Open only during fiesta, the family owned business sells only churros, rounded sticks of fried dough covered with sugar.

arise about the Fiesta program. A friend will have a copy of the official program and scheduled events. Few can imagine the wide range of activities available. The events held each day range from a display of brute strength in the woodchopping contest to a breathtakingly beautiful presentation of young girls singing traditional songs of the region. Official activities commence at dawn – when the town band,

La Pamplonesa, plays the first diana of the day – and continue until nearly dawn of the next day when the last of the officially sponsored musical performances on bandstands scattered throughout the city is unplugged.

The market is closed on July 7, the saint's feast day. Every other morning the market and its coffee bar are bustling.

During the mornings there are events in the bullring ranging from acrobats jumping over bulls to performances by musicians and dancers attired in costumes of centuries gone by. Perhaps the most moving ceremonies are the traditional pageants involving children. And one of the rowdiest events in Fiesta appears on no official schedule. It is the night of the drums. Round stickers announcing the night of the drums are passed out after the encierro on the day the organizers decide the event will take place. Every drum in Pamplona will be in Santo Domingo at midnight. A procession of pounding drums circles the city for a couple of hours, breaks apart and fades away.

IF you have wisely vowed not to make plans with others during Fiesta for fear you will break them, you may still make plans with yourself and promise yourself that you will attend some special event. You probably will break those plans too. But after a long night of partying and the tension of the encierro you really do want to make a decision about food.

The choices for meals in Pamplona are as overpowering as the chances for drink, that is to say, unending. Every place has food, every place has drink. Breakfast, like every meal, is a hard call.

Breakfast on Plaza del Castillo can be really expensive and pretty lousy. But sometimes there is amusing entertainment on the plaza at this hour as an impromptu comedy plays out when the water cannons of the street cleaning trucks aggravate people sleeping in the square. At this hour the army of the sleeping and those suffering hangovers is growing to battalion strength. Those making up this army of the dead are novices who don't know how or do not care to pace themselves. They have already self-destructed on the first full day of Fiesta. They may be among the crowd that goes through life burning the candle at both ends. Many who live this way say the lifestyle only makes their light that much brighter. But here in Pamplona they may find that the fire that lights their candle is hotter than any they have known.

About now, mid-morning, my closest Fiesta friends are usually at the stand-up bar in the public market, a place where the coffee is good, the conversation better, and one can pick up fresh fruit and other provisions for the hotel room. The city's bakeries are also excellent and crowded at this hour. In small restaurants on side streets and alleys local men serenade the crowd, singing jotas during breakfast where wine substitutes for juice and coffee. Those places are always crowded too.

Navarrans love to eat. Whatever you do about breakfast, it will last all morning. Every meal lasts a long time in Spain, even longer in Fiesta. The breakfast decision we made today was inspired. A few of us joined a group of Navarrans in a shaded street. Long wooden tables with table cloths and strong wine were laid with mountains of food: melons, ham, cheese, sausage, tortilla, a large rice dish, plenty of white asparagus, oranges and other fruit. Ten meters away another group sat at a long table, singing beautiful jotas. Our table was blessed with two excellent tenors. The singing at both tables continued throughout the meal. At one point we all paused to watch a parade of the *Gigantes*.

OPPOSITE PAGE: *Perhaps the man carrying the Cabezudo has been doing this for so many years that he has begun to resemble him. The cabezudos are part of the Court of the Giants which is comprised of eight Kings and Queens representing Europe, Asia, Africa, and the Americas as well five Cabezudos, six Kilikis, and six Zaldikos.*

The morning procession of the Gigantes makes its way through town.

These "giants" were created by a Basque painter in 1860 to carry on a tradition begun in the thirteenth century. The huge figures that originally danced through Fiesta were made of *papier maché* and represented things such as famine, pestilence, and war. At the end of the Fiesta they were tossed in a big fire with the hope that these things would not visit the village in the coming year. Now the Gigantes represent the continents of the world. In the fifties the figures were invited to Macy's Thanksgiving Day parade in New York. A photo of that time shows the black gigantes alone in the warehouse where they were stored and the picture carries a caption to the effect that these Gigantes were wondering where their friends had gone, for the black figures were not paraded in Manhattan.

As we sauntered through the streets following breakfast, we were drawn to a bandstand where a group of young musicians from San Sebastian played a stirring, brassy rendition of *Tiger Rag* and then featured their accordions on *Theme From The Moulin Rouge* while a mime troupe danced in front of the musicians. As I arrived at my hotel for a *siesta*, I found the front door blocked by a band of bagpipers dressed in Highland regalia playing traditional Scottish music.

My friends talked me into passing up my hotel one more time in order to tour two infamous bars informally referred to as The Bird Bar and The Mussel Bar, both located in an area commonly called the Aussie playground. Attending Fiesta is almost a rite of passage for Aussies and, once there, their custom is to climb to the top of a stone column in the center of this small plaza. Once they reach the top they stand straight up and fall over like stiff boards, free-falling into the arms of their countrymen who are as drunk as they are. Serious injuries occur when jumpers miss or catchers fail. As we rounded the corner a bloody young man was being loaded into an ambulance, another was readying to jump and three were in line, clinging to the monument. It was too messy for me and I wanted to siesta.

With the morning meal over, sleep is all you can think about. As you return to your room for a shower, you relish the idea of a long overdue siesta, the most civilized custom in a civil land; a long, quiet sleep through the afternoon. Soon enough though, you realize that you barely have time to change clothes and no time to sleep. It is almost time to go to the bullring for the *apartado*, the sorting of the bulls, and following that there will be the inevitable long lunch with friends, a meal of seafood and laughter. After lunch, everyone will linger at the table until it is time to go to the bullfight. And after the corrida it will be night again. Another enchanted night. Sometimes it seems sleep will elude you until Fiesta ends and sometimes it feels like Fiesta will never end.

Sleeping and dreaming are turned inside out in Fiesta. One dreams of being able to sleep rather than sleeping to be able to dream. As soon as you settle into

A father walks his son home after the parade of the giants and a morning pageant.

69

bed there is a wake-up call from the street. The uninterrupted succession of street noises varies in volume between muffled commotion and unruly cacophony. There are marching peñas, all brass and percussion, and drum corps that bang their way up the street, as well as the lovely melodies of groups of marching children playing fifes. In intervals when the music moves beyond hearing range the street fills with crowds chanting and singing. And always near are explosions of long firecracker strings that seem to stretch from the central plaza to the French border.

THE decision I reached was to attempt to skip lunch and sleep after the midday apartado, the ceremony of sorting the bulls that takes place in the corrals behind the bullring. The apartado was overcrowded as it always is in the beginning of Fiesta. The functional,

SANTIAGO LYON / ASSOCIATED PRESS

Tres toros at the apartado or sorting. The view from the bullring terrace at midday.

work-like process of sorting the bulls, moving them out of the communal corral to small individual paddocks, is elevated to the status of a social occasion for *aficionados*, people with knowledge of and a serious interest in bullfighting. The terraces behind the bullring are shaded by tall trees and overhanging roofs. Here people mill about and look over the corral containing the bulls. The scene at the apartado contrasts with the street. Here the people are nicely dressed and the *tapas*, small snacks, are tasty, and the sherry chilled and dry. It is hard to work your way through the crowded terrace to a railing in order to see the corral. If you are lucky enough to get a good look at the bulls and are in the company of a knowledgeable aficionado, you may learn a lot about bulls and hear informed opinions about which of the individual bulls may perform well in the afternoon corrida. Most everyone in our crowd will venture a guess about which bull will be the best in the afternoon, though among friends no one is ever chided about their erroneous predictions as all understand that bulls are invariably unpredictable.

This is the closest most people get to the bulls. Aficionados study the bulls' horns and their imposing physiques closely, as well as how they behave in the corral. These bulls probably were raised on the same range on the ranch where they were born. They were probably transported to Pamplona on the same truck though they were held in individual wooden crate-like containers for the journey. Then the bulls were together again, sharing the same corral across the river for several days, and then the corral at the beginning of the encierro last night. This morning they ran together in the streets of the encierro. Now, at the apartado they are together as a *manada* or herd for the last time. They will fight and die alone in the afternoon.

The end of the sorting process is often the most interesting part. Earlier in the day at a private meeting overseen by the authority of the bullring and attended by the bull ranch foreman and representatives of each matador, decisions were reached. After consultation, the fairest division of the string of six bulls into three equal pairs was decided. Once the pairs were determined, their brand numbers were written on cigarette papers, wadded into tiny tight balls and placed in a straw hat. The representatives of the matadors then drew lots to determine which pair of bulls their *torero* would face, and finally they advised the president of the bullring of the order in which the toros would appear in the corrida. What we witness at the apartado, is the physical sorting of the bulls, which are moved into small, single, box-like pens under the ring.

After the fifth bull is removed from the corral by following a steer to his individual pen, leaving the last bull alone, you have the only opportunity outside of a corrida to observe the behavior of a fully mature four-year-old fighting bull separated from the herd.

When left alone in the corral in Pamplona, many bulls go to the far corner of the large pen, a corner near a big tree that is near the gate where they entered the corral after the encierro. Those that don't have the tendency to look for that door or the way out, the ones that stand calmly in the center of the corral, unflinching, are normally bulls that prove to be good in the bullfight. Lingering on the terrace of the patio behind the bullring after most spectators have left, I looked down upon the last bull in the corral until an oxen led him away.

Bulls elicit strong emotions. When viewing a fighting bull in a closed corral, most people are struck by the power the animal possesses. The most impressive bull in an apartado is usually a quiet one, betraying no nervousness about his unfamiliar surroundings. Watching one bull standing alone quietly with a calm, confident demeanor, one sees great beauty and senses savage brutality.

To see these bulls in holding corrals, again as they trot across the river in the quiet night, and then to see them racing full out through the streets in the encierro, and finally witness their date with destiny as they go to their death in the corrida is an experience that leaves one feeling both full and empty at the same time.

In the end it is all about the bull. The bull is the central, unpredictable fact and focus of Fiesta. During Fiesta there are many quiet, polite conversations among well-dressed, knowledgeable aficionados which include detailed discussions about toreros, a term applying to all of the men who participate in the corrida, and matadors, the term reserved for those who kill bulls. These conversations are held under high ceilings in the cool, pristine marble lobbies and bars of elegant hotels and restaurants, especially in the hotels where toreros dress for the corrida.

Some hotels have taurine art exhibitions, and as I visited the exhibition in the Maisonnave and later had a drink at the Yoldi, I observed serious toreo discussions in progress. These conclaves are often academic in atmosphere and occur in a formal way after a corrida, as well as informally any time two or more serious aficionados are present. You will hear as much talk about the toreros as the toros in the discussions held in these indoor settings.

Things are different outdoors. Among the identically clad masses in Fiesta in the crowded cafés, if there is talk about the bulls at all, it is not conversation about the corrida or bullfight to come in the afternoon. The subject in sidewalk cafés is of those moments in the morning, the encierro. The amount of money you have, the price of the seat you can afford, determines how close you will be to the bulls in the afternoon bullfight. Courage alone dictates how close you are to the bulls in the encierro.

Pamplona's Fiesta is billed as *Feria del Toro*, the fair or fiesta of the bulls. It is one of the biggest bullfight fiestas in Spain, though several other ferias have more prestige and are considered more important in the taurine world. Other fiestas have their own distinctive, charming characteristics, like the tents and well-groomed horses in Sevilla's celebration, or the fireworks of Valencia's *Fallas*. In Pamplona bulls are the centerpiece.

It wasn't really necessary that I see the bulls this morning at the apartado. I had already seen them three times. Yesterday I spent a long time observing them in the holding corral across the river. This morning I got a glimpse of them for a few seconds in Santo Domingo. And last night I had the good fortune to have a ticket to view the *encierrillo*, the night crossing. Every evening the bulls are moved from the main corrals on the far side of the river across Rochapea bridge to the corral at the beginning of Santo Domingo.

While Pamplona prepares for the afternoon bullfight, life in the surrounding countryside continues as it has for centuries. A man works in a field, another tends to grapes on the vine, while two old timers idly pass time chatting. Leaving Fiesta and driving just a few miles out of Pamplona, you will be embraced by the majesty of the mountains and the charm of the region's farms and villages.

The encierrillo, a magnificent moment, takes place about an hour before midnight. The quiet of the night crossing is strictly enforced by the police who will carry a bystander away for making the slightest noise. The pace is far slower than the encierro and in a way the sight is more awe-inspiring.

The bulls share the street with steers, oxen and a few herders. The best place to watch is on the stone wall near the corral on Santo Domingo, looking down the hill toward the bridge, but one needs a pass from the authorities to have that vantage point. As the bulls cross the river and travel up the slope the only sounds are the clunk of the oxens' pongle bells and the dull clack of hooves hitting the road.

JOANNA B. PINNEO / AURORA & QUANTA PRODUCTIONS

JOANNA B. PINNEO / AURORA & QUANTA PRODUCTIONS

As I walked down a back street toward the hotel, I knew sleep was finally near and I had no doubt I could count on a wake-up call from Pamplona's marching bands, the peñas. With the precision of Big Ben, the peñas parade through town every day one hour before the corrida, waking me, allowing just enough time for a bath, shave and change of clothes before the bullfight.

Right on schedule music sounded like an alarm, rousing the city, signaling the coming of the corrida. After showering there is time to hurry to

Plaza del Castillo to get a glimpse of the dignified procession of devotees of *la fiesta brava*, the bullfight. Again La Pamplonesa provides the music for the formal parade from town hall through Plaza del Castillo to the bullring.

At the head of the parade are two stately, spirited horses ridden by the *alguaciles* of the corrida. The riders are dressed as officials in the time of Spain's golden age; black suits, plumed hats, and capes. As they walk slowly around Plaza del Castillo, La Pamplonesa plays *La Entrada*, a soft, gentle melody. The air of the procession is filled with cigar smoke and the smell of perfume, as well-dressed men and women follow the band to the bullring.

Behind the band several footmen lead a team of huge horses flying the red and green colors of San Fermín on their harnesses. The horses are on their way to work. They will drag the body of the bull from the sand of the arena to the butcher shop behind the ring, though recently – for the first time in Pamplona history – bulls were cremated rather than butchered, in response to fear of disease among cattle in Europe. The horses will have hard work to do as some bulls weigh three quarters of a ton.

The alguaciles are not just colorful, ornamental figures. They will assist the president of the plaza de toros from the moment they lead the formal *paseo*, the parade, which begins the corrida. The president will hand down the key to the *toril*, the gate from which the bulls are released, to one alguacil. The alguaciles will also award matadors the trophies ordered by the president when the torero triumphs; one or two ears, possibly a tail, conceivably a hoof.

As La Pamplonesa leaves Plaza del Castillo turning onto a narrow passage leading to the arena they begin to play *pasodobles*, beautiful, formal, traditional music written for the bullfight. The music floats across the town. Physically rested and spiritually restored, I begin to rush, for I know what comes next. In a few minutes this stately, organized procession will give way to the discordant notes and pounding bass drums of the peñas surging toward the bullring up Estafeta and through Plaza del Castillo.

At 5:30 p.m. on July 7 the peñas make their first formal appearance in Fiesta. For many this is the real beginning of Pamplona's annual party. Peñas are social clubs with their own meeting places, some of which are just tiny, unfurnished bars that only open for Fiesta, New Year's Eve and other special holidays. Other peñas have fancy facilities with swimming pools, tennis courts and amenities normally associated with a country club. Though each peña has a year-round social, cultural, and sports calendar, they exist primarily for the celebration of Sanfermines.

The oldest clubhouse on Calle Jarrauta belongs to *La Unica*, founded in 1903, and the newest group is *Peña San Jorge*, founded in 1980. The youngest peña has permanent headquarters in the San Jorge barrio, a good walk away from the old quarter where Fiesta is centered. So, like other peñas, it moves its base to a bar in Calle Jarrauta during Fiesta.

Membership requirements vary, but unless you are born into a group or sponsored by members there is not much chance of affiliation. There are no application forms. Each peña has its own crest sewn on pañuelos proudly tied around members' necks. Some, like San Jorge, wear special checkered smocks.

Once the peñas appear before the bullfight on the seventh, they never fade. Most peña bands play traditional music associated with Fiesta, but anything goes. One year a peña chose to play only Elvis Presley songs in the early hours, while another played only Benny Goodman tunes.

On July 7 all the members of a peña will parade either up Estafeta or through Plaza del Castillo, and their faithful follow them. They play the rowdy, rollicking, raucous, high energy music of the region. Each peña is led by a distinctive banner adorned with clever art work. Some *pancartas,* or banners, bear cartoons; others carry political or poetic statements. The last line of a peña is made up of strong young men carrying large boxes of food and industrial-size plastic trash cans filled with sloshing sangria. They will make their way to their honored positions, seats they have held for years in the sunny section of the bullring.

The large, tall, colorful banners dance in the air in a line stretching the length of Estafeta. The movement of the banners, a frantic swaying action, indicates the standard bearers are dancing with the same energy as those around them. As each new band rounds the corner it seems to drive the others to a fevered pitch. All peñas self-start, almost like spontaneous combustion, and they feed off of one another, each group trying to play more loudly and more strongly than the others. The energy and excitement of the dancers and musicians pulls people off the walls into the street like a magnet. Banners, banging drums and blaring horns converge at the bullring. Estafeta is the street where the bulls ran this morning. Now it is transformed. It is a place of danger in the morning, dancing in the afternoon.

THE time approaches to celebrate the nobility, bravery and wild ancestry of the bulls, characteristics which have been preserved through centuries of selective breeding. In the taurine bars near the bullring, it is a struggle to get to the bar for a drink. To communicate with a companion across the barroom, it is necessary to resort to hand signals as the conversations in the bar are so loud. The sense of anticipation of this crowd is infectious, and here, though hundreds of voices speak in a small place at once, the ambiance is cosmopolitan and genteel compared to the wild spirit of the peñas parading out in the street. Beautiful women in expensive dresses and men in starched whites press close to one another in the bar. Their conversations are punctuated by laughter.

The local aficionados who gather before and after the corrida in the taurine bars understand bullfighting, and this crowd is as serious as a group of opera fans might be moments before an opening night. This is the moment they have waited for all year. The corrida is their theater, their symphony, their opera, their art. In the bullring they will sit in the shade on the opposite side of the arena from the peñas.

Outside the bars near the bullring people are gathered on sidewalks watching the peñas make the final turn under the trees to march into the bullring. There is a high probability pickpockets are working the area. These thieves are part of a large Gypsy contingent that travels from fiesta to fiesta selling cheap flowers, telling fortunes, begging for *euros*, shining shoes and stealing money. The ticket scalpers are more independent and less organized than the Gypsies but no less professional and transient, and a whole network of them moves from one bullfight feria to the next. The fortune tellers, pickpockets and ticket scalpers are all part of the fabric of Fiesta. In the last moments before the corrida some female *aficionadas* buy flowers from the Gypsies, bouquets to throw to a matador following a moving performance. Others pick up food to share during the bullfight.

Once one arrives outside the bullring it is necessary to negotiate your way around long lines stretching under the tall trees, columns formed at the ticket windows which are almost always closed. Some fans will camp out in these lines for days, attempting to secure just one *entrada*, ticket, for one corrida. The bullring overflows every day, so finding a ticket can be impossible. An organization named *Casa de Misericordia* is responsible for organizing the fights, and they handle applications for season passes, *abonos*. It is an above-board, honest operation; fans granted abonos may rely upon receiving the same seats every year, though the waiting list for abonos is long. The law strictly prohibits the scalping of tickets and that rule is enforced by the police, if haphazardly. Still, if you are not concerned about the cost of an entrada, you need only to stand outside the plaza an hour before the fight and some character will approach you with a ticket for sale. Many of the bullfights are televised, so some days the option of watching from a bar rail does exist for those who are unable to obtain admittance to the bullring.

Entering the plaza, you walk along the concourse toward the portal of your *tendido* or section. Cushion vendors slam their wares on counters creating an echo like a repeating rifle and bass drums resound from stone walls like heavy artillery. In the midst of these competing sounds, you move to one of the bars, have a drink and hear the sound of more peñas storming the plaza. Business at the bars is brisk. Some small bars sell champagne and others have cigars, while the long bars have every kind of liquor. It is loud here, nearly deafening some days. There is no other bullring like Pamplona's and there is no other time like the last moments before a corrida during Fiesta de San Fermín.

Drink in hand, you move toward your seat only minutes before the corrida begins. If you are late the door to the tendido will be locked and you will have to be content with seeing only five bulls, for no one is admitted during a fight. If you are early you may witness the clowning of the peñas performing unscheduled skits on the sand before the start of the bullfight. Nothing is sacred to the peñas as they frolic before the fight. They make fun of the matadors, conducting mock parades attired in vulgar costumes with piles of wadding jammed in the crotches of their pants, and they have even made fun of the Pope. Their statements are sometimes more politics than parody. On opening day in 1994 the peñas unfurled a huge banner which read, "Three men who do not believe in God – The Mayor, The Governor and The Archbishop."

Not all of the peñas' demonstrations are frivolously rebellious. Each year on July 8 the peñas solemnly unfurl a gigantic banner and the entire plaza observes a moment of silence before the corrida. The ceremony is in memory of Germán Rodríguez, a young man killed during the 1978 riots which suspended Fiesta. The upheaval began in this bullring when the *Guardia Civil* fired tear gas and rubber bullets into groups of peñas demonstrating for the freedom of incarcerated Basques who they viewed as political prisoners. Most witnesses say the demonstrations that year were no different than prior years and that it was the police who provoked what ensued after they stormed the bullring. The riots spread to the streets, where fire, smoke, broken glass, overturned autos and the sounds of gunfire dominated the night. It was a tragic time for the province, a sad time for Fiesta, and the first time in the modern era that Fiesta was canceled.

Following the riots of 1978, a truce was enacted among all parties. In the fall of that year, the city sponsored a mini-Fiesta of three days as a test of the stability of the political climate. Everything held and no major incidents occurred for the next 19 years.

The truce was tested if not broken in 1997 when there was a 24-hour suspension or cessation of the celebration following the assassination of a public official in the province by *ETA*, a terrorist group that serves as the military wing of the Basque separatist movement. ETA struck out that July in retaliation against actions of the Spanish state which were the outgrowth of a series of events occurring over the previous year and a half. In the middle of Fiesta a handsome 29-year-old city councilman from a nearby town, Miguel Blanco, was kidnapped and assassinated. Millions of people across Spain turned out for demonstrations against ETA. In Pamplona, officials suspended all Fiesta activities for 24 hours, including a scheduled bullfight and an encierro the following morning.

In the middle of that night there was rioting in front of Pamplona's town hall that began when young thugs in sympathy with ETA set fire to pañuelos tied to an iron gate in a makeshift memorial to Miguel Blanco. Since then there have been no serious incidents but the presence of ETA is still occasionally felt in Pamplona, along with the more ominous presence of heavily armed, specially trained troops. ETA has escalated their war in the past several years and spread the violence to every corner of Spain, bombing cars, airports, government and commercial buildings. And on the last day of Fiesta 2001, at about the same time the rocket fired for the encierro a bomb exploded in a nearby town that caused death and destruction. That Fiesta could again go up in flames is a tragic thought no one wants to entertain, but all are aware of.

Though there are still anti-government slogans and inflammatory words painted on public walls in Pamplona today, most of the graffiti is more lighthearted, more in the spirit of Fiesta. Political sentiments are still expressed through the actions of the peñas and sometimes crassly, as when the whole mob in the sunny section of the bullring turned their backsides to the president's box and sang a ditty about how the mayor could kiss their rear ends. They were angry over some municipal policy affecting their organizations.

Today the sunny section of the bullring is a grand party. These days the peñas and the authorities seem to have an understanding that though some political protest and expression may be a part of the celebration, this event is too sacred to be marred by violence on either side. Only a minuscule minority in northern Spain, a group almost too small to count, condone the violence of ETA. And for ETA to attempt to politicize this celebration is foolhardy, for Fiesta is a representation and presentation of so many positive aspects of Basque culture, customs, and traditions.

O~NCE~ the peñas enter the bullring and find their seats, all bands begin playing at once. The sunny section is ablaze in blue and white, black and red, amid a cacophony of brass and pounding drums. As the peñas are situated directly over the pens where the bulls are corralled in the dark, they are dancing over animals who will die in this pageant, evoking imagery which harkens back to ancient sacrificial rites and barbaric rituals.

The bulls enter the plaza one by one, leaving their dark environs. The entrance of each bull is announced by a trumpet call, an echo of Roland's horn in the Pyrenees. If luck, skill and art combine in the corrida, then the afternoon will also bring forth music. The official band of the bullring will play a pasodoble when a matador is triumphing in the *faena* at the end of the fight, when he is alone on the sand, working close to the bull with the *muleta*, a small red serge cape. When the bull and man are like one on the sand, both exhibiting the best within them, when the bullfight achieves artistry, then from high above will come the stirring strains of famous songs written for the corrida.

In Pamplona's plaza de toros, it is the band director – and not the president of the ring – who determines whether the artistry on the sand is so meritorious as to be deserving of music. This makes the band director the most important critic in the plaza for the music heightens one's emotional response to what he or she is seeing. Though there is always raucous music coming from the peña section, formal music will fill the plaza when the matador is linking a series of artistic, difficult, long passes. This is when drama becomes art.

All of this may come in time. But now the peñas are in place in the plaza, whipping themselves into a frenzy while the matadors and the men of their cuadrillas await their parade, nervously adjusting their clothing and donning their formal parade capes. They smoke a last cigarette, say a final prayer in the chapel in the callejón, and line up according to seniority, all wearing the elaborately decorated capes they will drape over the wall in front of a patron or friend.

The bullring has two tiers, with stone columns and carved balustrades separating the *grada* or higher sections from the lower tendidos. The president's box is set off with bunting in the upper section, as is a much larger box with wooden chairs that is reserved for bull breeders. The president of the plaza and his two advisors enter in formal attire at the very last moment to signal the start of the pageant.

JOANNA B. PINNEO / AURORA & QUANTA PRODUCTIONS

Two members of a cuadrilla assist a matador as he dons an ornamental parade cape. In the background is the door to the capilla or chapel where the men say a final prayer.

In most plazas a bullfight is conducted in near silence before an audience that is as well mannered as those attending a symphony. Pamplona's plaza is always noisy. In other bullrings, a reverent hush falls over the crowd the moment the bull charges from the toril or gate, and again when the matador lines up the bull for the kill. Not so in Pamplona. Sevilla's *Real Maestranza Plaza* has the feel of an outdoor cathedral, while Pamplona's plaza de toros is often home to outrageously bizarre scenes reflecting Fiesta's many eccentricities. In the midst of a moving faena the peñas may begin singing a one word song over and over. In the early nineties one of the songs was "Induráin, Induráin, Induráin," a chant sung to the tune of *Stars and Stripes Forever*, and a reference to the legendary Pamplona cyclist, Miguel Induráin, who was then in the process of winning a record five championships in the *Tour de France*. Induráin retired from cycling but the peñas have not retired his song.

Induráin's major contribution to Fiesta was an odd, unintentional one, and nothing he had a direct hand in. For years the city fathers wanted to pave over the cobbled stones along the encierro route, raising the street to the entrance level of the stores, converting some sections to pedestrian malls. Preservationists, historians and prominent local bullrunners vehemently opposed the plan. Then came the year the Tour announced it would come into Pamplona and stay overnight in honor of Induráin.

"A-ha," said the city fathers, "We must pave the street for the cyclists in the Tour de France." There was even some suggestion or hope that the cobblestones would be uncovered when the bicycles left town, but that was not to be. The impact of the paving heightened the danger of the encierro and increased the likelihood of injury. The footing for the animals is treacherous some mornings when this surface is wet. In recent years even the steers who know the route well and normally navigate the course without incident have been slipping, sliding, and falling down.

When the peñas are not singing to their favorite cyclist, they may all sing traditional tunes or even *Happy Birthday* in Spanish, and often they break into a Latin rhythm while thousands stand on their

A major fan of Pamplona cyclist Miguel Induráin photographed during the Tour de France champ's heyday. Induráin is still just as popular in his hometown.

seats, shaking, bouncing and shimmying with the beat.

Some matadors have boycotted Pamplona because of the danger posed by the din and constant movement in one half of the plaza. One of the top matadors in the world, Jose Miguel Arroyo, *Joselito*, recounting being hit in the chest by a melon thrown from the stands as he faced a bull in Pamplona in the late eighties, said, "It's the only time I've ever felt ashamed to be a torero." Joselito now boycotts Pamplona's plaza de toros during Fiesta.

However, with the exception of Joselito and a very few others in the modern era, the best have come to Pamplona time and again, and many matadors choose to dedicate a bull to the rowdy fans in the sun, lure the bull to their side of the arena and kill it in front of them. It is true that to fight bulls in Pamplona is to fight under battlefield conditions, but a triumph in Pamplona is unlike a triumph anywhere else. The embrace of the public here is not reserved, it

Peña members dance in the bullring as multiple bands play rollicking music just before the start of the bullfight. Their clothes are clean, but that won't last long.

knows no limit. As a triumphant matador tours the ring, representatives of the peñas will climb onto the sand to present pañuelos, statues, wineskins and medals to him. Some gifts of the peñas are nonsensical, such as the Volkswagen car door handed to a young matador years ago.

THERE may be a *novillada*, a bullfight matching novice matadors with three-year-old bulls, or a *festivale de rejoneadores*, mounted matadors, before the first corrida of Fiesta on July 7.

During Fiesta, a total of 48 full-grown, four-year-old fighting bulls will be killed in Pamplona over eight consecutive days. These 48 bulls will appear in the encierro in the morning as well as the bullring in the afternoon, six bulls each day for eight days. Each corrida will feature six brother bulls from the same ranch. The names of the ranches and matadors scheduled can be found on posters and handbills.

Like matadors, the individual bulls all have names, though

most of them are ignored by all but the critics and photographers. Some names, however, are remembered among almost all aficionados: like *Islero*, the name of the bull from the *Miura* ranch that killed one of Spain's greatest matadors, *Manolete*, in the bullring of Linares, Spain in August, 1947.

Some runners and followers of the encierro may remember the name *Antioquio*, a *Salvador Guardiola* bull responsible for the death of two runners on July 13, 1980; one gored in the beginning of the run and another killed when Antioquio reached the bullring.

The symbol of the ranch and an identifying number is branded into the hide of the animal's flank, and the bulls fly the colors of their ranch in the form of a *divisa*, ribbons attached to the hide on the back of the neck with a small barb. The barb is placed by a man on a catwalk across the corrals underneath the plaza. He uses a long pole to insert the divisa when the bull leaves his holding pen and heads for the sand of the bullring.

The bulls of Fiesta de San Fermín are selected carefully. A serious effort is made each year to bring the best bulls from the best ranches to Pamplona. These plans are made at each of the bull ranches in the spring when six bulls are agreed upon by the *ganadero*, the bull rancher, and representatives of Pamplona's plaza de toros. The representatives also rent or buy substitute bulls to be held in their corrals on standby in the event they are needed.

Some bulls travel a great distance to Pamplona as many of the best ranches are concentrated in the south of Spain. Occasionally bulls shipped to Pamplona are injured in transit, in the encierro, or rejected by the inspecting veterinarian because of some defect.

In a recent year, an official statement was issued to the effect that the veterinarian rejected a whole string of six bulls because he "found insufficient bone content in the horns," a euphemistic way of saying the horns had been shaved, made shorter and more sensitive. Such things are not noticeable to the untrained eye and are often missed by even an experienced observer because of the great artistry of the men who use files to shave horns.

Every few years the discovery and public disclosure of incidences of this practice of unfairly handicapping the bulls causes a scandal in the Spanish bullfighting press. Some say the practice is only an occasional occurrence and others say some matadors will only face bulls that are shaved as closely as they are.

Horn shaving is almost as old as the corrida itself, and it is performed while the bulls are boxed for transit with their horns protruding between slats in the crates. Because of the amount of money involved in bullfighting, many millions of dollars, those who are at risk financially stand to gain by ignoring, covering up or sponsoring this practice and other practices which may handicap the animal or grant an advantage to the man.

While it is alleged that some bulls are drugged, the effect of administering medication to a bull would be fairly apparent while the impact of shaving its horns is more subtle. It is presumed that horn shaving impairs an animal in the same way a boxer would be impaired were his reach, the length of his arms, reduced by several inches on the eve of a match. Bulls use their horns by instinct. From birth on the ranch, young bulls joust with one another. Bulls know where their horns are, where the dagger points are, and how to use them. Some suppose that shortening the length and altering the tip of the horns all but neutralizes the chance of the bull effectively striking and sticking, though this is not fully supported by the evidence. The Miura bull that caught and killed the great Manolete, for instance, had shaved horns.

One matador I know refused to fight in a corrida when it was suggested that someone shave the horns the night before the fight. He told me when a horn is shaped artificially with a file, rather than naturally, it becomes razor sharp and it will deeply penetrate and slice anything it contacts. As many horn wounds have differing, changing trajectories after the point of entrance, it was his feeling that a shaved bull actually poses a greater death threat than a bull with its horns intact.

The scandals over shaving, the allegations about drugging and the complex and biased politics of the taurine world, a system which favors some matadors and ranches over others, are but thick, dark threads in the colorful tapestry of toreo.

Three picadors relax while exercising their mounts before the start of the bullfight.

One current contentious argument concerns the size of the bulls. The crowds in the north of Spain have for many years demanded big bulls with big horns. The size of the bulls in Pamplona has been a trademark feature of Fiesta. During the late eighties and early nineties the bulls were big everywhere, and there has been a lot of controversy about the mammoth size the bulls have grown to over the last twenty years. Some critics claim the bulls are intentionally overfed to create this crowd-pleasing bulk, and that this extra weight weakens their joints, muscles and ligaments and vitiates the animals' natural athletic ability.

Other critics have gone as far as accusing some ranches of breeding the very spirit out of fighting bulls today in order to provide a more docile, less dangerous animal for the matadors. At least one critic contends that ranches are catering to a newly affluent, mostly ignorant audience across Spain, people who have found a new

A bull enters the Pamplona plaza. The Toril is sometimes called the gate of fear. The weight of the bull, 560 kilos or 1,232 pounds, is displayed above the opening. To the right of the opening, wearing a green beret, is the man who receives the key to the toril from the president of the plaza.

pastime and believe that bigger is better in all things. Newcomers to Fiesta should not be overly impressed with the size of the bulls. Size is only one factor in the formula which determines a bull's value. In fact, if one examines the information on the brass plaques under the shoulder mounts of bulls that adorn restaurants, bars and hotel lobbies in Spain, one will discover that the great bulls memorialized this way, because of an extraordinary corrida long ago, weighed as much as a hundred kilos less than the average weight of a fighting bull today.

In Pamplona, all of the bulls you see will be huge and they will also be dangerous, though not all will transmit a feeling of danger. All of the matadors will be talented, though not all will transmit emotion in their performance. As in all art forms, for a corrida to succeed it must evoke emotion from the bull and the performance of the matador. Without this emotion, attending a corrida is an empty experience for both a first time observer and the most experienced aficionado in the plaza.

Some serious aficionados are there only for the bullfights and the balance of Fiesta is only a curious sideshow to them, something they have little interest in. These same men and women are at bullfights all across Spain throughout the *temporada* or season, which begins in February and lasts until late fall. They are in Sevilla in April, Madrid in May, Burgos in June and Pamplona each July. Some follow the fiesta circuit while others follow their favorite matadors, crisscrossing Spain and maintaining one of the toughest travel schedules imaginable, the travel schedule of a matador. Matadors are lucky if they arrive in Pamplona the night before they are scheduled to appear. Some do not arrive until the morning of the corrida.

ABOUT midday, the time the bulls are sorted in the apartado, the matador is in his hotel room. These men are paid handsomely and they stay in luxurious accommodations with excellent restaurants, though a bullfighter does not sample the cuisine of his hotel on the day of a corrida. He will have no noon meal beyond a light snack for he could be in surgery before the day ends. Some matadors will try to sleep through the early afternoon. Others expend nervous energy playing cards or chatting with old friends in their cuadrilla, the men who serve as *banderilleros* and *picadors* for them.

When the time comes, with the help of his sword handler, the matador will dress in the *traje de luces*, the suit of lights. It takes longer to dress a matador than a debutante. His suit is complex and to fit properly it must be carefully adjusted. Some matadors dress alone with only their *mozo de espadas*, sword handler, for company. Others like to have an entourage present.

As he dresses, a matador may hear the murmuring and the muted conversations of those who have gathered in the street at the front entrance of the hotel to offer wishes of good fortune as he departs for his appointment in the arena. And there are always more well-wishers waiting for him at the bullring as he arrives at the *patio de caballos*, the place behind the plaza where horses are kept. Men offer a pat on the back, women offer a kiss, and others hand over holy medals.

Every era has produced its *figuras*, though there is not universal agreement on what constitutes a figura. As the term is used here it refers to a matador whose presence dominates a period, one who captures the imagination of the public, if not the unanimous approval of critics. Some would argue that the title figura can only be bestowed upon a matador after the critics have deconstructed his entire career with emphasis on his performances in what are termed first class bullrings with particular brands of bulls. By any definition, most figuras have fought in Fiesta de San Fermín. But Pamplona's response to popular bullfighters has not always been in sync with the tastes of the larger public. An example of this occurred in 1965 when Manuel Benítez, who fought under the name *El Cordobés*, appeared on a cartel. He was famous around the world as the "Beatle of the Bullring," a reference to the length of his hair, and he was resoundingly denounced by some critics for his departure from the classic form. But he was a gutsy, flamboyant bullfighter, the kind of guy Pamplona crowds normally embrace. However, he failed to triumph and the crowd screamed insults at him and littered the ring floor with seat cushions and everything that was not nailed down. Undaunted by the abuse, El Cordobés stood tall at the edge of the sand, removed his shoes in the presence of all and slammed the slippers together, signaling that he did not want so much as a grain of sand from Pamplona's bullring in his shoes. He ultimately required a police escort in order to leave.

The list of Pamplona's favorite matadors is long. As the nineties dawned their new hero was César Rincón, a Columbian matador of extraordinary talent whose style harkens back to a purist, classical approach. On some days in Pamplona's plaza, Rincón put everything on the line, risked it all, and fought in the style of revered historical figures like Antonio Ordóñez. In his first appearances in the world's most important plaza, Madrid's *Las Ventas* bullring, he was carried out of the main gate on the shoulders of the crowd four successive times in one season, an unparalleled feat. Rincón, like Enrique Ponce and Joselito, emerged as a figura of the nineties. For several years these three matadors topped the popularity list with critics and crowds alike, then along came Jesulín de Umbrique.

By 1994 Jesulín was breaking records for the most corridas fought and most trophies awarded in a single season. He was distressing the purists and critics as much as he delighted the public. In a sense his career was a replay of El Cordobés' impact on bullfighting thirty years before. For a torero, Jesulín stands very tall and his short shock of dark hair gives him a stork-like appearance. He is irreverent about everything, including toreo. He has ridden motorcycles to plazas and laughed at things other matadors take seriously, and he fights bulls in a way which many feel is disrespectful to the tradition.

He has climbed on one bull's back, put another's horn in his mouth, hosted a corrida for women only, and carried on in the tabloid press like a male Madonna. Most serious aficionados believe Jesulín is vulgar but most grudgingly admit that he can *torear*, fight well. The public in Pamplona affectionately embraced him at the height of his popularity and just as quickly turned on him a few years later when he stopped doing stupid things like putting the horn in his mouth.

In a country where matadors are tossed flowers and hats as well as other inanimate gifts when touring the ring in triumph, Jesulín had infants handed to him in the bullring as if he had the power to bless them. That Jesulín was a phenomenon for a few seasons is beyond argument. When Jesulín entered the patio of the plaza in Pamplona on July 14, 1994, even the balconies and terraces overlooking the area were packed with admirers and curious onlookers. He entered like a rock star and the crowd, mostly women, hysterically mobbed him as reporters shoved microphones in his direction while camera shutters clicked. He had become a young millionaire and a huge star.

When his star faded in subsequent seasons, he continued to fight well and began to earn more respect. Then he suddenly retired at a very young age. In the 2001 season he began a comeback. He is still young and it is too early to tell whether he is just a flashing comet in the galaxy of bullfighting or something more. Probably – like many other figuras – his success offers a reflection of his time, and his early career stands as a commentary on an era when celebrity and publicity substituted for talent and ability in many professions.

The greatest matador of the epoch at the end of the last century was unquestionably Enrique Ponce, and it will not take time to determine whether his star shall shine forever. There simply is not anyone who does it better, more consistently or more artistically. He has triumphed in Pamplona but has never become a darling there. This may be because what he does, he does so well it looks easy, or because he has often had bad luck with the sword in front of this crowd, needing more than one thrust to kill the bull.

The Pamplona crowd is not as inclined to the art of toreo as they are to the valor of it. They want bravery and one of the bravest and most interesting matadors on the scene today is young Francisco Rivera Ordóñez, a kid who has a long suit in courage and a family lineage only a novelist could create. The consensus opinion is that the two greatest matadors in the world in the fifties were Antonio Ordóñez and Luis Miguel Domínguín. One is the grandfather of Francisco, the other was his uncle. His great-grandfather was the model for Hemingway's matador, Pedro Romero, in *The Sun Also Rises*. Francisco's father was *Paquirri*, a very brave torero who was gored to death when Francisco was a boy of seven. In all of the taurine world there is not even a fighting bull with a better bloodline.

When Francisco Rivera Ordóñez graduated to full matador status in Sevilla in an auspicious bullfight held on Easter, Resurrection Sunday, the whole taurine world held its breath. His performance was beyond belief; grown men wept, and he was carried on the shoulders of the crowd through the gates of one of the most important arenas in Spain.

After frustrating, unsuccessful appearances in Pamplona's Fiesta, Ordóñez had a triumph in 1998. The dramatic narrative of that corrida could not have been better scripted for the audience.

Ordóñez was so severely tossed by a bull, making direct contact with the horn so many times that experienced men in the audience thought he had been fatally gored. Miraculously, he was not killed – though he was seriously injured, and the horns had almost undressed him, ripping his pants to shreds.

Donning a pair of blue jeans cut off at the knees, with his shirttail out and tie askew, the Hollywood handsome young man proceeded to brilliantly and bravely torear until he killed quickly with one sword thrust. The crowd almost tore the place down and the president awarded two ears as the matador was carried from the ring to the medical facility in the plaza and then rushed by ambulance to the hospital.

In every sense Fran, as his friends call him, is different from many matadors who regularly appear in Pamplona. For one thing, with no fanfare at all, Ordóñez joins the locals in the morning and runs with the bulls. This young man, who runs bulls with ordinary men in the morning and dons the suit of lights and is the center of attention in the afternoon, married nobility

COLLECTION OF NOEL CHANDLER

Francisco Rivera Ordóñez in Pamplona

when he was wed to a descendant of the Duke of Alba. His is a story deserving of an entire book.

At the moment this is being written, Matador José Tomás is at the top of the heap in the eyes of almost anyone. There are always some critics with athletic intellects and flexible ethics who can mount an argument for or against any matador, but generally it is agreed there simply is no matador who can compare to Tomás. Some Spanish newspapers have put forth the theory that José Tomás is the reincarnation of Manolete and others have theorized that he is an alien, of another world. Only this young matador can hush the peñas in Pamplona with muleta in his left hand, preparing to do a series of passes known as *naturales*. If Tomás continues to fight this way for as long as Rincón, Ponce and Joselito have, his name will be mentioned with theirs long after his era is over. The odd thing about Pamplona's love for José Tomás is that his approach is cool and classical, and they normally are drawn to more fiery, histrionic matadors.

There are many good matadors today, older experienced toreros and young, up-and-coming bullfighters. It is a golden age in that sense. The sensation of the past few seasons has been a child torero, Julián López, known as *El Juli*. On the day El Juli made his first communion, he donned the clothes of a bullfighter and fought a young calf. At 10 he was in a school for bullfighters. At 14 he was participating in corridas in Latin America. As soon as he reached the legal age of 16 in Spain, he became a full matador.

El Juli does it all, everything but sell the tickets and beer. His work with the cape is acknowledged to be as good as anyone and it is done with a flamboyance not seen since the thirties in Mexico. He places the *banderillas* in the withers himself, thrilling audiences with his flamboyant style. And his work with the muleta and sword are excellent. From his first corrida all of Spain was in love with him, including the peñas of Pamplona. It has been Juli the past few seasons, and not the older guys, who has been selling out plazas. If Juli does not burn out, a danger many worry about because of the way he pushes himself day after day, he will push José Tomás for the title of torero of the present epoch.

Though he has a baby face and is still in his teens, El Juli has been the sensation for several seasons and his annual earnings are in the millions of dollars. Here he triumphantly tours the Pamplona ring, adorned by panuelos tied around his neck by members of peñas, holding the ear the president awarded him.

Though all bullfight fans believe they know something about what it takes to be a matador, no one but a matador will ever know what the last, final moments before a corrida feel like, for the matador is the last man to live by the sword. It is true that soldiers willingly risk their lives for pay and freedom fighters lay it on the line for their cause. Others knowingly risk their lives on a regular basis by engaging in high risk occupations. None but the matador engage in scheduled, contracted lethal combat, announced by a *cartel* and attended by critics and thousands of fans, and then attempt to create art in the process. Only a matador makes this kind of appointment and keeps it.

A leading matador will have more than a hundred bullfights during a season that lasts approximately 240 days, and sometimes he will appear in as many as four or five corridas in a single week. Those that appear this afternoon in Pamplona will leave tonight, traveling overland by car – or by private jet in the case of the leading toreros – to another city for another appointment tomorrow afternoon.

To them tomorrow's business seems far off now. All that matters now is now, this corrida in Pamplona. No other art form possesses this almost overwhelming feeling of immediacy.

Every corrida is the culmination of years of devoted work by many people. Some have worked their whole lives for this moment, their lives being entirely dedicated to toreo. These people work in a tradition centuries old, presenting a glorious ritual. This is the only artistic pageant played out in a furnace of fear, a place where art is welded, fused, melted and then gone forever.

Many foreigners, including some famous writers, have tried to view this spectacle as a sport when there is nothing at all sporting about it. The word sport implies a game or a contest with a winner and a loser. There is nothing more serious, dangerous and deadly than a bullfight. The outcome is certain in that the bull will die. The matador may be killed. Only in the rarest circumstances will a bull live. Only a bull that has shown exceptional bravery and dramatically displayed extraordinary characteristics will have its life spared. That decision is made by the president of the plaza.

There are no winners and losers in a corrida. There is danger for the man and death for the bull. A lot of brave men have died from horn wounds suffered on the sand of the bullring. Years ago men died agonizing deaths when the original horn wound was not sufficient to kill them. They died of horrible infections which spread through their bodies.

The horns are long, sharp and often roughly splintered at the tip, and nearly always encrusted with excrement and filth picked up in the fields and corrals. Deep horn wounds were once always deadly, but since the invention of infection-controlling drugs and the development of advanced surgical techniques and modern means of transportation, the possibility of surviving a serious horn wound has increased. At the entrance to the bullring in Madrid there is a statue of Scottish Dr. Alexander Fleming, the man who discovered penicillin.

Deaths still occur in toreo when horns pierce men's hearts or other vital organs. Matadors, banderilleros and picadors have all been killed or gravely wounded in recent seasons. Two talented banderilleros, Ramón Soto Vargas and Monolo Montolíu, died on the horns in the Sevilla bullring during the same season and two accomplished and experienced matadors' careers ended about the same time when they, too, were tossed by bulls. Though the horn did not pierce either matador, both suffered crippling spinal injuries and paralysis. One, Julio Robles, lived on quietly in Spain for several years before his death while the other, *Nimeño*, ended his own life in suicide when he was unable to recover sufficiently to fight again.

If toreo may be compared to any other artistic endeavor, perhaps it is theater. The bullfight is like a three-act play that follows a prescribed form, though the narrative is unpredictable. It is also kind of like an evanescent ballet or music heard from afar. Technically it is about the matador's physical relationship with the bull. Artistically, it is about his metaphysical relationship with the bull, himself, art, and death. Unlike painting or sculpture, it is impermanent, difficult to photograph, preserve, or recount. When it is over, all that remains is the mute signature of the art form, blood on sand.

Occasionally the bull will dictate the script, though more often it is the matador. The story line is begun by the ganadero, the bull breeder, who made the most critical decision years earlier far from the bullring, a decision to match a certain cow to a certain stud bull. In the end, if a fighting bull lacks what aficionados call *casta*, the possession of desirable characteristics obtained genetically, even the most brilliant matador will have trouble fashioning an artistic faena in the final act of the drama. In large measure it is the bloodline which scripts the performance of the bull. Bulls from certain ranches often share similar characteristics.

The principal player in the drama is the matador, a man who has devoted his whole life since boyhood to this art form. His performance, though scripted in outline form, will mainly be interpretive, possibly impromptu and sometimes wholly unscripted.

In regard to the composition of a corrida, there are almost always three matadors matched with six bulls, two for each matador.

In rarer festivales, the rules may be altered and one man may face six bulls alone, or two men may split six bulls in something called a *mano a mano*. Mounted matadors called rejoneadores may be involved in separate corridas or included in festivales. When bulls from different ranches share a card, it is called a *concurso*.

In a corrida when three men fight two bulls apiece, they rotate in order of seniority beginning with the first to graduate to the rank of full matador in a ceremony known as the *alternativa*, an event that marks the first time a torero leaves the novice tier and alternates

Matador Pepín Liria, a favorite in Pamplona, opens with a traditional pass, a verónica.

with full matadors rather than novice bullfighters. In the event of a serious injury to or the death of a matador, the senior bullfighter remaining is charged with dispatching the animal that inflicted the wound that disabled the torero.

W HEN a bull is released from the toril, it will usually run loose on the sand for a few moments. Some bulls leave the gate cautiously, tentative about their new surroundings. Others recklessly blast into the sunlight, scattering sand beneath their hooves. The matador's cuadrilla will attract the bull's attention by flinging capes over the *burladeros*, protected openings in the wooden barrier circling the sand. As the bull runs and reacts, charging the capes, sometimes slamming into and splintering the red planking of the burladeros, the matador studies its movements.

Each bull is different. Some favor one horn over the other. No two bulls have the same vision, or move with the same speed, and rarely do two bulls respond identically when they first enter the arena. Ideally, a bull should run smoothly with speed toward the cape and hit the wood head-on without hesitation, striking with both horns.

The first act of the pageant begins when the matador, holding a large cape, steps from behind the burladero onto the sand. He attracts the bull's attention and begins to make passes, mostly *verónicas*, passes named for the saint who wiped the face of Christ.

These early passes should be long ones, sending the bull away a good distance after each encounter, conditioning the animal for the faena to come. As the bull attacks, the matador changes terrain, moving the animal toward the center of the ring, thereby beginning to dominate him. Ideally a bull enters the arena in a wild, unmanageable, dangerous and outright savage state only to gradually become more graceful without losing its primal instincts.

Variations of verónicas, the lovely passes which bring the bull through long gentle advances to and through the cape, are performed in the beginning of the first act. If these passes are done well the bull should make long charges, head down, horns lowered, following the cape during the charges. The matador should move the

The sensation of recent seasons, El Juli, opens with a series of passes from his knees, fighting in a style called tremendista as the peñas chant "Ju-li! Ju-li! Ju-li! ...."

cape at the same speed as the charge, just inches in front of the horns. At the end of each pass, as the bull goes through, the matador should "send it away," making the charge as long as possible. If the passes are short, choppy, and hesitating at this first stage of the fight, it is likely it will be difficult to fashion an interesting or artistic faena.

Slowly the man begins to take control of what was an uncontrollable beast moments before. He also gains control through his actions between passes. As the matador steps toward the center of the ring, he lures the animal from the terrain it has chosen to defend. A backpedaling or retreating matador cedes his power. It is important that the man dominate early and throughout.

The president signals for the trumpet to announce the entrance of two mounted picadors. The horses and picadors who enter in the second scene of the first act are important players in the drama in the sense that bullfighting on foot as we know it could not exist without picadors. The enormous lumbering horses used in Pamplona are blindfolded, their ears plugged. They wear heavy protection and are injected with tranquilizers. For centuries cavalry mounts had their vocal chords cut so that their screaming in combat did not add to the confusion of unnerved men. Nowhere have I read that these horses have their vocal chords cut, but I've never heard a horse cry out in a corrida.

The matador will gracefully bring the bull to a position to charge the horse, a little over a bull's length away. This is accomplished with beautiful passes that at times appear like a series of interlocking circles on the sand. The picador cites the bull with his lance and the animal charges into the heavily padded horse and onto the steel-tipped lance that sticks into an area just behind his neck. The better the breeding, the more the bull will push through the weight of the horse, ignoring the pic. Some feel that the initial contact creates a feeling of fulfillment in the bull. Until the moment the horns and head of the bull hit the horse, its only target has been the cape which should have eluded it entirely. When the horse is hit the fighting bull engages an enemy full force.

The exertion of the bull pushing against the huge horse weakens the bull as much as the loss of blood from the wounding with the pic. If the bull is not slowed in this manner it cannot be fought. Some bulls make contact and shy away, and others chop at the horse. Bulls with the best breeding will charge the horse in the same way they charge the cloth, without hesitation, pushing straight through.

The matador moves the bull away from the horse between pics with a series of passes called *quites*. The bull will receive three or more pics. As primitive as the practice appears, it is actually a very delicate art. When done well, it can make a good bull better. When done poorly it can destroy an animal physically and spiritually and remove the very essence of its inbred instincts.

This phase of the corrida has never been popular with the foreign audience though serious aficionados study the animal's behavior carefully at this time. In Pamplona, picadors are sometimes abused by locals who attempt to toss fruit at them from the sunny section. Occasionally, but rarely, they do hear the applause they deserve for a difficult job well done.

THE trumpets sound again on order of the president, signaling the second act, the beginning of the ballet of the banderillero and the bull. The bull is armed with two huge horns. The man has two skinny wooden sticks, both wrapped colorfully, sometimes in the colors of the bull ranch. Each stick, or *banderilla*, is about two feet long with a metal barb on one end.

The man will stand a good distance from the bull and cite a charge, usually by jumping or showing some movement. The slightest movement should provoke an attack from a toro bravo.

The bull charges, running full out. The man dashes also, running in a quarter circle, sticks held high above his head. The line the man takes and the line of the charge of the bull intersect, the bull's horns aligning with the man's body.

Over the horns, the sticks are placed in the *morrillo*, the hump behind the bull's head. The bull and man run on. In the moment when the man goes over the horns, the danger of death to the man is obvious. A man who does this for a living and does it well is an artist deserving of the highest regard. No other stage in the world presents art rivaling this dangerous dance with death.

There are matadors who place the sticks themselves and are better known for placing the sticks than placing the sword, but the vast majority of banderilleros are not active matadors but rather members of a matador's cuadrilla. Some of the best cartels have been those featuring two or more talented matadors placing their own sticks like the battles between Víctor Mendes and El Fundi, corridas that often had inspiring, memorable results.

As the second act begins, the bull has already charged a large cloth cape and then slammed into a big horse several times. Now the bull runs free on the sand in pursuit of a human target. This act is traditional and probably originated in the acrobatic bull dances of Crete.

JOANNA B. PINNEO / AURORA & QUANTA PRODUCTIONS

Sol y Sombra, sun and shade. A symbol of the corrida and all of Spain. As the sun begins to set behind the plaza, the corrida takes on a Picasso-esque look.

Three sets of banderillas are placed. Sometimes all will be placed by the same member of the cuadrilla or by the matador himself. During this act the matador will have a last opportunity to observe the bull and note its tendencies. A bull in shock from pic-ing will sometimes be revived by racing after banderilleros. As the sticks are only an arm's length, the bull comes close to catching the man three times and can be invigorated by the near misses.

Some banderilleros and picadors become famous within taurine circles. Many aficionados know the name and toreo history of every member of a matador's cuadrilla. Though in the end the light shines on just one player in the drama, the star, the matador, the way his cuadrilla performs will have a major impact on the outcome of the corrida. For the finale or faena the matador will be alone on the sand with the bull. Until that time, he shares the stage with his supporting cast, the members of his cuadrilla.

Crowds have their favorites among cuadrillas, though many just cheer banderilleros and jeer picadors. Nowhere are picadors more rudely treated than in Pamplona, though it is silly for one to scorn a picador because whatever he does is done at the direction of his boss, the matador.

Pamplona loves banderilleros. They have an all-time favorite, a fellow who was built more like a picador than a banderillero, a man with amazing agility and ability. Though rotund, he was fond of wearing bubble-gum colored suits which were far from figure flattering. They loved him so much in Pamplona that they called his name all afternoon when he appeared.

For years after his last appearance in Pamplona the crowd continued to chant his name for sentimental reasons even when he was not in the plaza. They would chant his name loudly when other banderilleros failed to perform to his standard. When others failed to place the banderillas on bulls that were particularly difficult or especially dangerous, this man seldom missed. They sang his name to the heavens when he planted the banderillas between the horns. He was known as *El Formidable*, and today his talented son – who strikes a similar profile – performs the same role in the corrida.

Bullfighting obviously has a lot to do with bravery. Among those who sit in the sun with the peñas, bravery is appreciated over art ten to one. These people love *adornos* or flourishes, unnecessary gestures that some matadors might use to embellish a performance, like touching the horn or kneeling with their chest just inches from the bull. The peñas also love contrived gestures like a matador making passes on his knees, fighting in a style generally called *tremendista*. Purist aficionados believe the style to be vulgar and they frown upon such things except in the rarest

OPPOSITE PAGE: *The art of both the Banderillero and photographer John Kimmich-Javier are exhibited in this image of a pair of banderillas being placed in the second act of a corrida.*

instance, while the Pamplona public seated in the sun demands these gestures in excess.

THE faena is the finale. This is the most meaningful, most dramatic and most tension-filled act. Everything to this point is but a prelude.

After the last set of banderillas are placed, the bull is lured to the far side of the ring and all of the men, except the matador, withdraw. Only one man remains on the sand with the bull. From his sword handler he takes the sword and muleta, a red cloth much smaller than the cape he held in the first act. After formally asking the president's permission to kill, the matador may dedicate the bull to an individual. In Pamplona the *brindis*, dedication, is often made in the center of the ring signaling to all in attendance that this performance is dedicated to them.

Like this image, the corrida does become a blur of motion and color and the art of it is often found in the movement of the mammoth animal with long horns against the slight figure of the man with a cloth and sword.

Now – with only a small red cloth and sword in his hands – for ten minutes man and bull will remain alone on the sand. If things go well their images will appear to blend into one.

There are no rules for the faena. In fact, one of the greatest matadors of all time, Juan Belmonte, once said, "I do not know the rules, nor do I have rules, nor do I believe in rules." Each matador has his own style. Some are innovative and distinctive, others more an imitation of what has gone before, and some, like the tremendistas, are considered aberrations by purists.

Essentially, all matadors accept that the object of the faena is for

Two horns, six sticks.

the matador to utilize various styles of passes – some high, most low, some right-handed and others left-handed – all linked to have the bull "fixed" in the muleta and causing the bull to repeat on command.

With the muleta in front of him, the matador cites the bull, his leg straddling an imaginary line, exposed to the horn. As the animal moves through the pass, the man bends his wrist, extending the trajectory of the target and sending the bull away in a long arc.

Then, turning toward the bull, he will keep the muleta in the bull's face, out in front of his body. He will step into the imaginary line of the bull's charge, cite the bull and shake the cloth again. In this fashion the man will continue receiving the bull in long, graceful, sweeping passes very close to his body. Through every pass only the bull's legs should move, as the matador's feet should be still, planted in the sand. When the faena is good, the plaza will hear the band play pasodobles, and when it is really good even the peñas may suspend their playful nonsense and pay attention.

The final act will end in death when the matador meets the bull's charge head-on and plunges his sword between the bull's shoulders, severing the aorta and bringing death to the bull. The

spot the sword must strike in order to cause a quick death is about the size of a quarter. Going over the horns a matador must make an almost surgical strike, positioning himself in a posture where the bull's right horn is inches from the man's heart. Ideally, the bull's death is nearly instantaneous.

EACH of the six bullfights will proceed and end in much the same manner. After the death of the third bull, the midpoint of the corrida, most of the peñas leave their seats and go out onto the terraces, stairwells and concourses that ring the plaza. There they picnic. Some groups cook on grills with open fires and the fare may be sausage, chicken, seafood or huge dishes of *paella*, the spicy saffron rice dish that features everything but the kitchen sink.

Plates, glasses, buckets of beer and bottles of wine cover the concrete floor. Groups sit in large circles, generously sharing food and drink with passersby. They are oblivious to the bullfight and occasionally the entertainment they provide is more creative than that being furnished by the corrida.

By this point the peña members' white clothes are all but ruined. The men and women are soaked to the skin with the sangria, wine, champagne and beer they have poured over one another throughout the bullfight. Their skin is as sticky as it is wet, gooey from the pieces of fruit thrown between them and laden with the residue of the confetti, saw dust, flour and chocolate powder they have thrown at one another in the mad frolic which passes for fun in the *grada sol*, the upper sunny section of the ring.

When the picnic ends, it is nearly time for the peñas' afternoon dance, which commences when they return to their sections for the end of the corrida and the beginning of their parade into the night. They will dance through town all night and in their exuberance they

Though there is beauty in the corrida, there is also brutality, and the power of the bulls is ever present.

will also hug you. Being hugged by a member of a peña in this condition results in your clothes carrying decorative, discoloring debris, some of which never washes out.

The feast on the terraces and the alcohol consumed during the

DESMOND BOYLAN / REUTERS

ABOVE: *After placing a pair of banderillas, a banderillero finds himself in the bull's sights.*
RIGHT: *This matador escaped serious injury; however, the next day a colleague was gored through the neck.*

DESMOND BOYLAN / REUTERS

Late in the corrida flour flies in the peña section of the bullring, settling on clothes drenched with sangría and covered with chocolate powder, pieces of fruit and scars left by the direct hit of sandwiches.

bullfight fuels the peñas for the time when they take over the Fiesta. Though there is music during the day, it's nothing like the night. Because of the number of peña bands playing in crooked, narrow alleys and small streets, at night you can't tell where the music begins and the echo ends. After the corrida, the night will belong to the peñas.

DEATH is ugly for any living creature, including a fighting bull. Often it has been written and said about humans that it is more important to remember how one lived than how one died. As death is a part of life, it may be equally important to examine how one dies. A writer once said that if we know how one died, we will know how they lived.

Dignity in life is as beautiful as death is ugly. To live and die with dignity is the ultimate achievement for any creature on earth, and it is incumbent upon each of us to afford every living creature the same dignity in both life and death that we feel we deserve.

Animals have long been utilized as a food source for humans. Countless species have been captured, caged, penned and forced to live a life of absolute indignity before dying in assembly line fashion. In this time of taming, of consciously breeding out all undesirable genetic instincts and characteristics in animals, there exists but one breed in captivity that is allowed to live free to adulthood, enjoying majestic natural sur-roundings, growing with its dangerous wild instincts intact.

The toro bravo is one of the most aggressive animals on earth. It runs to battle and fights brave-ly. These bulls die as they have lived. If there is cru-elty in the corrida and there sometimes is, there is also honor.

ONCE they are killed, the bulls are dragged by a team of horses to the patio adjoining the ring. Presently they are loaded onto trucks and taken to a place where they are burned. Before the livestock disease scare across Europe, the animals were dis-posed of in a much different way.

Men working with long-handled axes and hatchets split the animals open, spilling blood across the cement and spewing hot steam into the air. It was a sav-age scene. The butchering procedure was startlingly swift. The crea-ture that appeared indestructible minutes earlier disappeared into unrecognizable shapes in moments. The butchers in rubber boots squished through the blood and running water, continuing their conversation which had little to do with their work and almost no reference to the bullfight. There might have been an occasional remark when a bull was brought out without an ear, evidence of a trophy awarded to a triumphant torero. Other than that, they talked about the things co-workers usually chat about: work, family, the previous evening and plans for that night.

The butchers always finished their work quickly and again the cement was spotless. Near the butcher shop in the patio are flower

ABOVE: *With the muleta in his left hand, El Juli executes a pass known as a naturale. The bull is "fixed" in the muleta, and the matador stands his ground.*
RIGHT: *Having dominated the bull, El Juli kneels and touches a horn in a gesture known as an adorno. Purists consider this a vulgar statement, though the masses across Spain who adore El Juli might disagree.*

DESMOND BOYLAN / REUTERS

pots with geraniums and as soon as the butchers finished loading the carcass onto a refrigerated truck, the whole picturesque scene again resembled a postcard of Spain.

The bull carcasses used to be trucked out of the plaza and distributed to meat packers and ultimately markets and restaurants. In the past in Pamplona there were places where one could eat bull stew and other parts of the beast, and that still holds true today, though the bull meat you eat may not come from a fight you witnessed.

Some love the meat, others find it has a gamy taste like that of a deer that ran to its death, producing adrenalin after being wounded. Regardless, the fresh meat was never worth much in comparison to the cost of a live toro bravo. A string of six bulls from a leading ranch can cost a bullring more than the price of a comfortable home in Spain.

Boom, Boom, Boom! The drums of the peñas begin to bang as the corrida ends. The bullfight is over and the chaos of Fiesta begins again. The peñas scramble down to the sand, all brass and drums. Outside, thousands line the street waiting for the bands to emerge.

One spectator covered in grimy, wine-stained clothes congratulates a matador following a corrida. The fan wanted a hug, but got a handshake.

Matador Jesulín de Umbrique riding high at the peak of his career.

In the bullring the peñas are forming into a parade. The ring fills with seat cushions tossed from above. The matadors and their cuadrillas make their way out of the plaza, threading their way through the peñas. Handsome toreros accept kisses from girls and slaps on the back from boys. The peñas are invigorated. Now they are again the center of attention. The night is theirs.

Most of the spectators drift out of the bullring and head toward their favorite bars. Back at Plaza del Castillo in the vicinity of Bar Txoko, the peñas parade past their families and friends. Small children are handed by wives to husbands in the bands. Some kids ride on their fathers' shoulders in the midst of the peñas. Young boys and girls are allowed to carry the banners and some are handed horns and drums.

Seeing this moment on this corner provides one with an unforgettable memory, a deeper feeling for Fiesta, and a fuller understanding of what the celebration means to those who call Pamplona home. The pride of these people in themselves, their families, their province and their Fiesta is authentic and never better illustrated than when the children join their parents in this grand parade toward a place where they will all dine together.

Slowly I cross through the peña parade and make my way to an outdoor table at *Bar Sevilla* on Plaza del Castillo. All the peñas pass by, strutting their stuff. The music reverberates as many bands play in the plaza simultaneously, their music colliding in the air and falling on us in fragments. A young friend stops by, searching for a ticket to the night crossing. Other friends walk by offering invitations to dinner. I thank them and defer.

It seems everyone in Pamplona wants to be a drummer. Though this child has his own instrument, he wants to play his father's.

I have other plans. Tonight I am going to sleep, and tomorrow I'll be as dangerous as a secret weapon. That's my plan. I have broken the rules and made a plan. Never mind. I believe I will keep this plan, for I desperately need more sleep. Other than my brief siesta after the apartado today and the nap I took during the fifth bullfight, I've had no sleep since yesterday morning. Quietly I stand and slip out of the plaza, bound for my bed in the hotel.

THE fire bull! I run head-on into this strange sight as I turn out of the plaza. As I reach Estafeta the fire bull, a man-made contraption showering sparks, becomes a suelto, turning and charging directly at my position. I join the runners, all little children, none of whom are waist high to me.

As these kids run noble and brave and stay close to the falling fire, I lurch into an awkward sprint for safety. Having embarrassed myself in the presence of a bunch of little children who got great joy watching me scamper away from the fire bull as a valiente, I decide to forego sleep a while longer and melt back into the crowd.

The night is lighting. Standing on the steps of the passage to the plaza I look back to the street. The sparks of the fire bull, powered by a man running beneath it, shoot straight up, illuminating the Basque flags draped across the center of Estafeta. Behind me a cheer goes up as strands of thousands of lights are turned on over Plaza del Castillo. Dancing in the plaza is about to begin. Similar scenes with formal stages for musicians are also set up in Plaza Consistorial, Plaza de San Francisco and Recoletas. Across from the bullring, open-air bars have cranked up their music to an ear-splitting decibel level, and hundreds of other bars are following suit.

I plan to walk across Fiesta toward Barrio San Juan to an area which is normally quiet, the Bosquecillo gardens, which are transformed during Fiesta into blocks of booths and tents serving food. The eating is good there and cheap compared to the prices demanded in the city center. The booths offer everything from chocolate *churros*, a fried sugary pastry, to whole meals built around roasted chicken.

At each end of the wide street bordering the booths and food tents are stages from which hard rock music screams out of mammoth concert speakers, drowning out the traditional Fiesta songs coming from small, nearly antique speakers mounted on tent poles. Groups of punkers, pink hairs, and neo-Nazis flash their cheap jewelry and discount ideology in the same street where young lovers embrace.

Why I wander in the direction of Barrio San Juan and the food tents is pretty much beyond me. A gang of friends asked me to join them as they headed for the tents from the bullring. Now that I have decided not to go to sleep, I guess I will join them for a feast of dead chicken. I'm certainly not hungry. In the bullring this afternoon I happened to sit in the lower section of Tendido 1 in very ritzy company. In keeping with the tradition in Pamplona's plaza, everyone brought food and drink for a light meal after the third bull. This meal, *la merienda*, was actually a full four-course affair among some wealthy aficionados in the most expensive seats.

Today the group in my row offered shrimp on toast, salmon, cheese, thinly-sliced ham and fruit, all complemented by the best wines Navarra offers. Afterwards an elderly man passed around excellent cigars while his wife distributed delicate pastries. All around me people ate beautifully prepared appetizer portions of ham and cheese, sausage and bread, fish and shrimp. Spain's bars call these appetizers *tapas*, but in the bullring they are known as banderillas, perhaps because they stab at one's hunger pangs.

Knowing I want to go to Barrio San Juan is one thing. Knowing how I will get there is another. Tonight, July 7, is the first full night of Fiesta in the sense that all the peñas are in the streets and a whole city and at least a town's worth of foreigners are out in the streets as well, and they will be out all night.

Immediately I scratch off Calle San Nicholás and Calle Jarrauta as possible courses to travel through the sea of people. In the early afternoon, during the corrida, Jarrauta is almost empty and it is a great time to drift through any of its dozens of bars. Nighttime is different. Nearly every peña has a clubhouse or bar on Jarrauta, and tonight the street will be impassable and Calle San Nicholás will be impossible. San Nicholás will be packed almost all week long.

I decide to swing wide and walk along the boulevard named for the great composer Sarasate. The median of this street is a Fiesta lottery center where chances are sold on everything from automobiles and motorcycles to tricycles. The eyes of young children, teenagers and young adults are all focused on the gleaming prizes. I play a game of chance I don't quite understand and buy a raffle ticket for a tiny car. Then I turn toward the fairgrounds.

Set near the bus station is a century-old carnival. The attractions here include carousels, roller coasters, games of chance and of course food and drink.

The huge ferris wheel has obvious structural defects. Bolts and braces are missing and what remains is rusted. It is as exciting and treacherous as any carnival ride in the world. I know brave bullrunners who are too afraid to ride this high wheel that offers one of the greatest nighttime views of the city.

The carnival has to be one of the loudest patches of ground in Europe. It is going strong when I pass it about 11 p.m. and it will still be going strong at six in the morning when it ceases operation for a few hours. The fair pauses once a day, and then only long enough to reload with a new shift of workers, more prizes and foodstuffs.

While the carnival rides swirl through the night with their neon lights and peñas storm through the streets like commandos with no intention of taking prisoners, there are well-dressed people attending a quiet cultural event in a theater named for the Basque tenor Julián Gayarre, who was born in nearby Roncal. Others are in art galleries viewing exhibitions of painting, sculpture and photography. All of that activity is indoors, as are the many fine restaurants that are serving at this hour.

Fish from the streams, rivers and private ponds of the Pyrenees are a renowned delicacy of the region, along with shellfish from the port town of San Sebastián, doves from the fields, and the lamb dishes for which the Navarrans are famous. And of course there are Rioja wines. The outdoor places and neighborhood cafés, places without tablecloths, with only wood tables stained by the wine of many seasons, offer a very different fare tonight.

There the fare is far simpler, the Navarran version of fast food: sandwiches, French fries, pimentos and ice cream cones. Tonight you cannot enter the finer dining establishments without a reservation, and without a world of patience you will not be served in the ordinary cafés. So you wander along the garden, beside booths where huge hunks of ham hang on strings, alongside the sausage stands, near the rotisseries of the chicken joints.

San Sebastián, only a 45-minute drive from Pamplona on a superhighway through the mountains, offers a great respite during or post-Fiesta. The best tapa bars in northern Spain are in a barrio near the harbor and the nightlife is invigorating.

Along the way there is always music. The music of this night is every music on earth: the traditional txistu music one would expect, but also salsa, reggae, folk, rock, swing, heavy metal and always the rowdy, pounding rhythms of the peñas playing songs of Sanfermines. It is all part of a beautiful and curious culture.

During the days, in the folklore exhibitions, one can glimpse the customs and traditions of these proud people, some of whom have always been separatists resisting the notion of being governed by anyone other than themselves. In a real sense a separate state does exist, separate from Spain and the rest of the world. It is a separate spiritual state.

The people of Pamplona love the natural beauty around them, a love which is evidenced by their many parks and their preservation of the walk along the old wall of the city looking down to the Arga river and the foothills in the distance. In this city once called *Iruña* and then *Navarrería*, ancient customs are preserved, even archaic competitions such as heavy stone lifting. The delightful *Día del Niño,* a day of Fiesta reserved for children, stands in sharp contrast to that he-man event.

With all there is to see and do in Pamplona during Fiesta, there is still always a day when my friends gather after the encierro, make a run to the market for provisions and leave for an outing away from Fiesta. Traveling to the nearby coast, you can choose between the aging, beautiful town of San Sebastián and the charming French seaport of St. Jean de Luz a few kilometers away.

Traveling south, you can take the road to Olite to visit a wine-growing region that was once home to kings, a place which has one of the largest castles in northern Spain, now converted to a lovely

Navarra's high country can be even more restful than the coast.

hotel known as a *parador*. Another road leads to Estella, a medieval city on the pilgrimage road to Santiago de Compostela. Journeying northward into the Pyrenees, all roads lead to enchanted settings.

The mountains have picture perfect picnic places, settings that resemble etchings in fairy tale books. High in Roncesvalles pass are secluded spots under tall trees beside narrow brooks, places illuminated with dappled and varying light which changes the tint of the mossy surfaces. White wine chills in the streams in minutes. In the shade everything chills. After a feast, if you have had the presence of mind to borrow bedding from the pensión or hotel where you are staying, there is time to cover up for the most peaceful sleep of the week, a siesta which ends in time to return to the plaza de toros for the first bull.

Thoughts of picnics, places I may go, things I might do later in the week give way to the present as I quicken my pace, veer away

JOANNA B. PINNEO / AURORA & QUANTA PRODUCTIONS

For the Gigantes, Cabezudos, Kilikis, Zaldikos who parade through Pamplona, Fiesta finishes the last day at the bus station when the children of Pamplona come to wave goodbye. Here a tired cabezudo and his companion rest. OPPOSITE PAGE: *Medieval villages, historic churches and former royal residences such as Castle Bitron are all within driving distance of Pamplona. Many such destinations are suitable for a relaxing day trip or overnight stay away from fiesta.*

Every night at 11 p.m. fireworks fired from the citadel light the sky.

JOE RIEHL

from the circus area of the carnival grounds and walk alongside the walls of the ancient citadel. I know I will be joined later in the week by one who loves the corrida, processions, peñas and fireworks but has little tolerance for the continuous noise beneath our hotel window. My wife, Melony, is one who subscribes to the theory that Sanfermines is a great fiesta for a woman, but no place for a lady. She is spending the first part of this fiesta in Florence looking at art, and she is already talking about finding a hotel for herself next July in the countryside near Pamplona, a place where she says one might get a civilized night's rest. She's got this fiesta figured out pretty well, for she will not arrive in Pamplona until Thursday when her favorite matadors appear.

A SOUND like a cannon suddenly drowns out the noise of Fiesta and everyone in the street cheers as the night lights up like a torch, creating an almost surrealistic sight as fire erupts from behind the tall, thick walls of the fortress. It is as if a long-dormant volcano has come to life. These are the fireworks of Fiesta, elaborate pyrotechnic displays that occur each night in the hour before midnight.

Just outside the citadel wall, fifty meters from the launching pad I find a place to lie on my back as fireworks glow and thunder high above me. Several blocks away in Plaza del Castillo, and in some of the narrow streets of the oldest barrio, the fireworks are reflected in topfloor windows of tall buildings, but the best place to see them is here at the point of origin.

OPPOSITE PAGE: *Thousands carry candles in the plaza in front of the town hall at midnight, July 14. The closing ceremony is as different from and dramatic as the opening at noon of the sixth.*

The sky is like the palette of an inspired artist: pinks, greens, golds, reds, blues, silver and bright white mix together and break into shards, accompanied by sounds resembling a military bombardment. As fireworks dance in the sky and thousands of small parachutes drop multi-colored flares, the crowd gasps. I am here again, in Pamplona in July. The first full day of Fiesta was good. There is no way of knowing what the days to come will bring, but I believe I know how it will all end eight nights from now. It will end as it always ends.

At midnight July 14 thousands will crowd into the town hall square, all carrying candles. Rockets will fire from the balcony of the Ayuntamiento and fireworks will explode over Fiesta a final time. There will be music and some of it will be sad.

Revelers on their way home will approach the gates of the great San Lorenzo church and place candles on a ledge at the arched doorway leading to the saint's chapel. Some will tie their pañuelos on the wrought iron gate at the entrance to the church, symbolically making a last offering to the saint.

All across the city candles will burn on café tables and curbs, small altars in a giant shrine. People will rise from tables at outdoor cafés on the plaza, down their last drink and stroll toward bed. I will wait in Plaza del Castillo for the last peña before dawn, believing that just before sunrise a band will appear to lead me out of Fiesta. Just as I always follow the music into and through Fiesta, I always want to follow the music out of Fiesta.

The time between the closing ceremony and dawn is a time when the city is eerily quiet for the first time in nine days. If I am lucky the night air will be shattered by the rumble of drums and blaring horns, and music will once again echo off of old stone walls.

In the somber silence, the last peña before dawn sounds out like summer thunder sent by the saint. Falling in behind the last peña, you wrap yourself tightly in the masquerade for as long as it lasts, following the peña until they reach the gates of the city and begin their descent down the hill toward the river bridge.

When the last peña plays the last song of Fiesta, you dance for the saint, for Fiesta, for absent and fallen friends, and for yourself.

Standing on the ramparts facing the foothills, you watch and you listen as the last peña moves into the distance, fading into the dawn. One drum continues to sound faintly. It is the sound of this distant drummer that will beat in your heart until this time comes again.

HEMINGWAY'S LEGACY

LEGACY

A LOST GENERATION, DRIFTERS, AND PERIPHERAL AMERICANS

1923-2002

AN AMERICAN SAGA:

An essay tracing the continuum of the American experience in
Sanfermines from Hemingway's first fiesta to the present.

HEMINGWAY'S LEGACY

A Lost Generation, Drifters, and Peripheral Americans
1923-2002

NOT EVERY FOREIGNER WHO GOES TO PAMPLONA is Ava Gardner, Errol Flynn or Tyrone Power, stars of the movie adaptation of *The Sun Also Rises*. One would think this is the case in reviewing much of the writing on the subject. Attempts to portray foreigners in Fiesta, especially Americans, have been works of fiction or other writings that should have been classified as fiction. Years ago Hemingway and Michener wrote novels with fiesta as a romantic background and those impressionistic works are as accurate as most of what has appeared in newspapers, magazines, books and film since then.

Fiesta is one of the most romantic settings on earth, but the reality of the foreign experience in Pamplona is that the drunks are not as clever as Hemingway's Mike Campbell; the good guys are not as good as Jake Barnes; and the wayward women not as lovely and beguiling as Lady Brett Ashley. It is true, however, that today one is not at a loss to find some dysfunctional Americans doing impersonations of these dysfunctional characters created by an author who was no stranger to dysfunction himself. One could pen a short piece about some of the Americans in fiesta and title it "The Sun Also Sets."

Hemingway got it right. The Fiesta is generally celebrated in a clean, joyous way by the local Navarrans to whom the celebration belongs. For foreigners who carry all kinds of baggage into town, the experience can be a medieval carnival with both light and dark sides.

Always in writings about Americans in Fiesta, it has been romance that carried the day and undoubtedly that will be the case here, though there will be an effort to strike a balance and present an accurate portrait of the American experience. Over the past thirty years, since Michener's publication of *The Drifters*, the majority of purported attempts to realistically portray Americans in fiesta have been in newspaper and magazine stories, portions of books, television news clips and documentaries, most of which fell into a predictable pattern. One who checks the facts contained in many of these pieces quickly learns that most of them do no more than feed a myth-making machine and reinforce the stereotypical image already engraved in the imagination of most Americans. Much of the writing amounts to little more than ego embellishments and often it is the writer's ego that is massaged most. It is hard to trust any of it.

It seems exaggerations are the rule, not the exception, among Americans in Pamplona. Many exaggerate the number of times they have been to Pamplona, the number of times they have run with the bulls, as well as bumps, bruises, knicks, scratches, and minor run-ins with a horn. A kind of inexplicable compulsion overcomes some Americans in Pamplona who seize upon fiesta as an opportunity for self-promotion, and writers often act as their shills, making them out to be what they imagine a Hemingwayesque figure is. The tradition may have begun with Hemingway himself who exaggerated in the news dispatches he filed from Pamplona and in letters to friends like Ezra Pound.

Part of Hemingway's genius was that he could make one faint pencil mark on a canvas, turn it toward us, and we saw a full-sized brilliant oil painting. His painting of Sanfermines in *The Sun Also Rises* is just that, a faint line made with a pencil. A line so brilliantly drawn that many still think of that book as the definitive work on fiesta, though one could not find the answers to ten basic questions about fiesta in those pages. It is an impressionistic work of the highest order, arguably one of the greatest works of fiction by an American writer, yet there is little factual information about what most think the work contains, the fiesta in Pamplona. Hemingway was a regular in fiesta during the twenties, but he never wrote about Pamplona again in any book after 1926, and he only went back to fiesta on two occasions after 1931.

Nearly fifty years after Hemingway's novel, James A. Michener gave us a Pamplona chapter in his treatise about Spain, *Iberia*, and in a novel titled *The Drifters*. Michener, like Hemingway, used fiesta as a backdrop behind the stage where some of the drama played out. Hemingway had only been in fiesta three times when he wrote a book that would forever identify him with Pamplona and Mr. Michener had made but one trip when he wrote *Iberia*. Thus, any misinformation or missing information can be readily understood and accepted. For the most part, these American writers were dealing with fiction.

The current crop of English speaking journalists who visit Pamplona fall into a pattern as a general rule. They roll into town, watch one bullrun from a balcony, sit on the plaza for a hour with an adrenaline-addled American who, fresh from the encierro, is eager to bend their ear. They have cognac, coffee, and conversation. Then they write and file "the whole story" of fiesta, and move on to their next assignment or join in the nonstop partying. The oft-interviewed Americans, "the usual suspects" as some refer to them, fellows always finding their way into television reports, newspaper and magazine articles and books, are people who obviously love the bright lights and attention. Some of them are good ambassadors for fiesta. Others sound a lot like pro athletes giving locker room interviews with well rehearsed "mike bites," repeating the same standard lines time after time, staying on message the way a politician does.

To be fair, the chaotic nature of the event is a contributing factor, accounting for some of the lapses in the accuracy of what is reported out of Pamplona. On the whole the majority of American writing on this subject continues to be unreliable accounts where accuracy and truth appear more as coincidence than as a constant.

The most untrustworthy information about Fiesta and Americans in Fiesta is probably that found in first person accounts people have posted on the Internet. With rare exceptions, these postings push the envelope in terms of being self-indulgent.

If one is to use the Internet to search for accurate information about Fiesta de San Fermín itself, then one should visit a website that is not American, but Navarran, *Sanfermin.com*. This site is translated to English and is produced by The Kukuxumusu Drawing Factory, a Pamplona based group founded in 1989. On this site Kukuxumusu sells a book titled *204 Horas de Fiesta* that has been translated to English and is the best guidebook a tourist will find dealing with Fiesta de San Fermín. The website and guide book provide accurate historical and contemporary information about fiesta itself.

It is much more difficult, nearly impossible, to find accurate information about Americans in fiesta in a historical or contemporary context. The image of Americans in fiesta that began emerging in the mid-twenties with the publication of the Hemingway novel is an image which has been reinforced for almost a century. For better or worse, myth married fact long ago, and this marriage continues to celebrate its anniversary each year on 6 July in Pamplona. What exists is a mountain of misinformation, ego-driven first person accounts, outrageous falsehoods, and some incredibly romantic versions which all serve to distort the reality of the American experience.

T HE story of the American experience in Fiesta de San Fermín is a long one, stretching back nearly eighty years to the time when Ernest Hemingway first arrived in Pamplona. He was not the first English speaker to go to Fiesta; several British and American citizens had been to Pamplona before 1923. However, generally it is Hemingway's novel that is credited with announcing the existence of the event to the English speaking world. When Hemingway went to Pamplona upon the recommendation of Gertrude Stein, the fiesta had already been going on in one form or another for centuries. After his novel, the celebration was to be interrupted once by a civil war, another time by rioting, and once briefly because of terrorist activity in northern Spain, yet Fiesta always endures and it flourishes today.

Hemingway's contribution to Pamplona is still a subject of controversy among some locals because his book brought us into town - - our money, our arrogance and our ignorance of the local culture, traditions and customs. However, still today, the American influence in Pamplona is arguably equivalent to the influence one infinitesimal droplet of coca-cola has on a huge cask of Rioja wine.

Though there are thousands of Americans in Pamplona every July, they are swallowed up by the masses of Navarrans and other nationalities. Despite preconceptions one might naturally have about this American group, there is no specific type in this crowd. The list would include men, women, children, bullrunners, singers, scholars, soldiers, dancers, students, hardy drinkers, sloppy drunkards, true and faux philosophers, movie stars, poseurs, accountants, painters, poets, lawyers, journalists, filmmakers, investors, war heroes, pacifists, authors, pilots, wits, bores, and even some of the bums of the masquerade.

Today the best of the bunch of Americans in fiesta, the undisputed stars of the American experience are nameless to this author, unknown to all but their friends. They are young people in their late teens and early twenties. They seem to come to Pamplona from every college campus in the United States. Their motives for coming to Pamplona the first time are very different from the motives many older Americans have for returning year after year. The kids come for the sheer fun of it, with a set of expectations not grounded in experience, armed with great reservoirs of energy. And though it all begins as a freeform dance for them, some will embrace the Fiesta in a romantic waltz and fall in love with Pamplona. For the rest of their lives most of them will count the memory of this romantic adventure separate and apart from recollections of other vacations, ski trips, dive trips or foreign travel.

Beginning on the day when they are normally celebrating the independence of their homeland, July 4th, a full two days before Fiesta, the advance guard of this legion is in evidence at the bus depot, train station and in the streets of the old quarter searching for rooms in small hotels, pensions or family homes. They can be seen standing in small groups, dressed in T-shirts, shorts and hiking boots, turning a map this way and that, trying to get their bearings among the crooked cobblestone streets.

Some head straight out to the campground outside town which will become a multinational mini-Woodstock kind of setting as Fiesta gets underway. Most meander through town, some holding quart bottles of local beer, others struggling with wineskins not yet cured and made worse by the quality of the wine poured into them. They gravitate to the route of the bullrun which looks harmless on this normal shopping day, take a look at the bullring that appears from the exterior to resemble a football stadium for a small college, and some make a toast to the large bust of Hemingway that overlooks Pamplona from its perch on Paseo Hemingway.

Many of the young ones head for the small plaza they have all heard about, the one informally referred to as the Aussie Square, easily the rowdiest English-speaking place in Pamplona. It is here, in the plaza where the Aussies hangout, that young Americans will soon be able to observe the absurdly reckless sport of street diving. Drunken young foreigners climb to the top of a tall pedestal in the small plaza and then freefall through the air, trusting their inebriated mates will catch them before they crash onto cobblestones littered with broken glass.

In the days before Fiesta there will be no street divers, no catchers and nothing at all remarkable about the small plaza where several streets converge. In fact, there is nothing out of the ordinary the young Americans will notice about any part of the city in these days before Fiesta or even in the final hours before the opening ceremony that will give them any hint of what is to come.

Some of them have a rendezvous to keep from an appointment made weeks earlier over a bottle of wine with new friends met on the Spanish Steps in Rome. Others have college friends they've promised to meet. The majority are traveling Europe in small groups of two to four persons, riding trains on rail passes and staying in youth hostels.

A young reveler jumps from the tall pedestal in the place many call "Aussie Square." All eyes are on the high flier except for the Spaniard at the base of the statue who poses for the camera.

Like the other rites of the Fiesta, this has become a ritual of its own: the invasion of young, smiling, laughing Americans who are in town to live fiesta to the max. Where once they could be seen in outdoor cafes writing postcards home, they now take numbers and stand in line in Pamplona's Internet cafés. Some even say they journal on computers in the cafés rather than writing in a notebook. As high-tech as e-mail communication and computerized record keeping can be, when they step back onto a cobblestone street and leave cyberspace behind, they step back into another time with traditions stretching back hundreds of years.

Every few years the complexion of this group of young Americans changes, reflecting the current state of a generation's culture and values. The heavy drug scene which once existed among foreigners in Fiesta has all but disappeared. Even the heavy drinking which is still a mainstay among older Americans in Fiesta seems to be passé among backpackers who now search out natural juices in the same way prior generations used to hunt for hashish in the sixties and seventies. As light as they travel, many carry their own music and walk the streets wearing headsets plugged into an audio player on

SANTIAGO LYON / ASSOCIATED PRESS

The young sleep anywhere, anytime. At midday there is a respite, and some parts of town are empty and quiet. The wise ones rest at this time because bedlam will rule again in a few hours.

their belt or in their pack, moving to a beat they alone hear.

No one has a firm estimate of how many thousands of young Americans are in Fiesta each year. Some only float through Pamplona for a few days before moving on to other locales in Europe. They are quickly replaced, however, by battalions of reinforcements. The scene at the bus depot and rail station is unchanging during the days and nights of celebration, and it seems there is no place in Pamplona where one cannot see or hear American college students.

It is obvious that Fiesta opens its arms to them. Many experience a temporary adoption by Navarrans who take them to their bars, show them their Fiesta and open their homes to them. Most young Americans swear they are coming back to Pamplona the next year and every year thereafter, and some keep that promise. Others have to wait many years before returning, and they report a sadness each July when Fiesta plays out without them.

There are young ones from nearly every nation converging on Pamplona by the time fiesta opens. There are large contingents of Swedes, Aussies, Brits, French, Germans, Dutch and other nationalities who have been well represented in fiesta for as long or longer than the Americans, and in some ways their presence is more pronounced. Among those nationalities as well as among the Yanks, there has always been a constant group, young and old, who make an annual pilgrimage to Pamplona. Some first backpacked into Fiesta a few short years ago. Others have been attending Fiesta for ten to forty years or more. The other nationalities tell their stories well. This essay is limited to a retelling of stories that define the trace of the American continuum in fiesta, and not all American stories can be told here because of space limitations and the nature and focus of this essay. Some stories we will miss out on are good ones like the chronicle of the first American who ran with the bulls. He was the U.S. Consul posted in Barcelona in the late forties, and was accompanied to Pamplona by the famous American author, Barnaby Conrad.

Noel chandler is the Godfather of the American experience today. Of the legions of foreigners who have made the journey to Pamplona, few have been as remarkable as Noel Chandler.

In the 1920's, Gertrude Stein proclaimed that Hemingway's fiesta mob was part of a Lost Generation. Fifty years later James Michener called foreigners in fiesta The Drifters, and one of the most extraordinary of their lot, Matt Carney, referred to himself as a Peripheral American. No one has yet given a name to the thousands of young Americans who crowd the transport stations and campgrounds each July, but someone will. Noel Chandler is not part of a lost generation and he is neither a drifter nor a peripheral American, or even an American at all.

Hemingway was a writer who enjoyed irony and he would love the irony that his successor as the most prominent English speaking person in Pamplona some seventy-five years following the publication of *The Sun Also Rises*, is not an American at all, but a proud Welshman. Of all foreigners who are in Pamplona year after year, Americans and others, Noel Chandler is the most impressive, most respected, and best example a young person could aspire to emulate.

Chandler knows as much as any foreigner has ever known about Spain, the province of Navarra, the city of Pamplona, Fiesta de San Fermín, bullfighting, bullrunning, the history, traditions, wines, food, music, religious rites and customs of this proud culture in the foothills of the Pyrenees Mountains.

Long before Chandler became the Padrino or Godfather for the foreign experience in fiesta, he was the center of a social agenda of sorts. Years ago Chandler hosted elegant breakfasts after the encierro at Hotel Tres Reyes. When the last breakfast event took place, Chandler gave medallions of San Fermín to those who had been regulars at these functions. Today one still sees foreigners and Spaniards alike wearing this beautiful medal around their neck during fiesta. It is a symbol of the Saint and also a reminder of another time and the unbounded generosity of Noel Chandler. His graciousness in hosting the gatherings at the elegant hotel was but a precursor of even greater generosity when he opened his home in

EDWARD GANS

Noel Chandler

Pamplona to guests and inaugurated the tradition of the Chandler champagne party held at noon on 6 July. Corks popped opening champagne, as rockets fired opening fiesta.

It is not Chandler's longevity that accounts for his position or rank as the present day leader of the legions of Americans who have followed Hemingway to Pamplona nor is it his knowledge of all things Spanish that sets him apart. Noel Chandler is universally respected because he is a gentleman, a vanishing breed in fiesta and the world at large.

Were Chandler aware that anyone was describing his place in the American or Anglo experience in these words, he would deny the mantle was his. If the mantle were thrust upon him, he would shuck it to the floor like a dirty shirt. He is a private person who neither seeks nor wants attention and would dismiss this kind of recognition as *caca de vaca*, a Spanish slang term that roughly translates to droppings of a cow.

For much of his life, Chandler was an international businessman who lived in cities all around the globe. Today he lives principally in Madrid. His greatest passion is the corrida or bullfight. Half of the year he follows the same punishing travel regimen of a leading matador, traveling day after day, crisscrossing Spain, following his favorite bullfighters. His passion for bullfighting caused him to follow Matador Antonio Ordóñez from Spain all the way to South America.

Forty years after Chandler followed Antonio Ordóñez, on the occasion of Antonio's grandson, Francisco Rivera Ordóñez's greatest triumph in Pamplona in which he was carried from the ring and rushed to the hospital, a corrida described in the preceding section of this book, Antonio's grandson kept the two ears he cut under his hospital bed in Pamplona until Chandler arrived that night and he could make the formal presentation to him. In November 2001, Francisco Rivera Ordóñez appeared in a bullring in Venezuela that was inaugurated by his grandfather in a corrida Chandler witnessed long before the younger matador was born. Following the fight in South America, Fran Ordóñez boarded a plane to attend a banquet in London with Noel. Chandler's knowledge and love of the art form is equaled by his loyalty, in this case extending to three generations of toreros in the same family, including Fran's father, Paquirri, a famous matador who died a noble, brave death from a horn wound when Fran was a boy.

Though he does not talk a lot about toreo or the encierro, there is no question among critics and afficionados that Chandler knows as much about bullfighting and running the bulls as anyone. Chandler would be the first to tell you that the encierro is something that belongs exclusively to Navarrans and bullfighting is something that belongs exclusively to Spaniards, and thus it is silly to talk about the knowledge of any foreigner in respect to either. However, he would be contradicted by both outstanding matadors and extraordinary local bullrunners, men who know him well and would say he is the exception, the foreigner who does know and understand these things the way the Spanish do.

Noel Chandler is not a Hemingway character. In some respects he may well be the kind of man Hemingway wanted to be. He adopted Spain and that ceremony was reciprocal, for Spain considers him one of their own. Anyone seriously interested in Fiesta and how one should conduct oneself as a foreigner in Pamplona need only look to the example of this Welshman.

O<small>NE</small> following in Noel Chandler's footprints is Tom Turley, a young American. If Chandler is the Godfather of the American experience, Tom Turley was kind of a mascot fifteen years ago when he wandered into Pamplona with a college friend. After fifteen fiestas, he is now one of the most well-known, well-liked Americans in town. The great Navarran runners have taken him into their embrace, not only because of what he does day after day in the encierro, but because of his character, personality and spirit.

In his first Fiesta in 1987, Tom was on the verge of turning away just after arriving in the plaza, discouraged by the crowds, the prices and the inconvenience of camping on the outskirts of town. He was later to say that he now believes he and his friend, Lynn Dorsey, were just overwhelmed by the massive and surreal sea of red and white in motion, swirling around them. As he was about to turn toward the bus station and exit Fiesta forever, he fell into a small group of Americans seated at a café on Plaza Castillo. Within an hour Tom and Lynn were given a corner suite in Hotel La Perla with balconies overlooking the plaza. They were handed excellent entradas or tickets to the week's bullfights, all free. The room and tickets had been abandoned by an American called home on business. The businessman had entrusted the paid up hotel suite and tickets to a friend of his for just this purpose – to bestow them like a lottery prize on a young backpacker who otherwise would have found himself sleeping in a park and scrounging for lousy tickets to the bullfights.

This was Tom's introduction to the generosity of Pamplona and some of the Americans in Fiesta. His positive personality, engaging manner and enthusiasm soon had him developing close friendships with American veterans and locals alike. From those friends Tom learned something of the encierro and fiesta that first year. He has become fluent in Spanish and has immersed himself in the culture of Navarra, getting to know other towns and villages in the province as well as he knows Pamplona. He lived for a time in Pamplona, teaching English and assisting in coaching the La Unica Peña in rugby. While living in Pamplona in 1992, Tom seemingly met every-

Turley in the thick of it. Wearing his lucky red shirt with white and green stripes down the sleeves, Tom is running on the horns of one bull and is focused on the bull in front of him as it begins a u-turn maneuver. A well-known local runner, Chema Esparza, was hit in the left leg by the bull's right horn but eventually managed to straighten the bull out and get it back on course.

one in the town. The Mayor has hosted Tom and his friends on the balcony of the town hall for the closing ceremony. Today, shopkeepers call his name when he strolls the streets, and it is rare when traveling the streets with Tom that you are not stopped by a local wanting to embrace him.

Turley is now completing work on a graduate degree in Denver. Prior to that he earned his keep working in humanitarian relief efforts in Africa, South America, the former Soviet Union, North Korea and eastern European nations caught in war. Some years he has had to fly to Pamplona from far-flung places and at times only made it on a wing and a prayer, but he has never missed Fiesta since his first year. Each summer after Fiesta ends, Tom tries to stay on in Spain so that he may participate in other encierros in northern Spain. During a recent summer he ran the bulls 28 times. His widely recognized ability as a bullrunner, his ease with the language, and his gregarious charm have made him popular.

Tom laughs and scoffs at the notion that he is a good bullrunner or whether that should even matter for he understands, as the Navarrans do, that talking about the encierro in terms of any kind of individual achievement is silly and contrary to the spirit of the event. Typically it is only foreigners who make much over how they have run. Turley is atypical in that he is more like a Navarran than an American both during the encierro and afterwards when he shrugs off anything anyone has to say about how his run was. He would be the first to tell you that there have been mornings where he has chased tails, mis-timed his break for the center of the street and been left in the position of a spectator. And there are many photos that show him in the aura of danger, on the horns, racing up Estafeta on days when it all came together.

Alone in the center of the street, Turley picks up a bull coming off of la curva.

About running, this young but very experienced American offers, "I love the risk, the excitement, adrenalin, chaos. It's a way to confront some core feelings, passions and perceptions, an incredible sensation. A unique experience. A peak experience. Some say it is spiritual and in a subconscious way it may very well be this for me as well. The camaraderie means a lot, a sense of belonging in the street now that I have friendships with other runners. In the street before the rocket fires, it is an interesting mix of casualness, chatting with friends, combined with a high level of mental focus and intensity for me. I am just lucky to be out there with the only people who really do run with the bulls, the locals. They can teach you, generously give you all they know over a lot of years, and then you watch them and feel you know nothing. And I love the bulls. To be that close to bulls for that time gives me a feeling I don't know the name of. It's the only time I ever have that feeling or combination of feelings. It seems like you are with the bull for a long time, but it's just moments." Those words would echo the sentiments of many who participate in the encierro day after day, year after year.

Tom Turley lives Fiesta fully. Though he loves the encierro and principally comes to Pamplona to run with the bulls, some days he passes on the encierro and goes to a mountain village to spend time with friends who live there. And though this Boston-educated New Yorker is as full blooded as any American can be, his Fiesta is lived almost entirely on the Spanish side. Like Chandler did years ago, Turley crossed over and is hardly a foreigner any longer in this town so familiar to him. In the streets of Pamplona for most of the day he wears the traditional whites with a pañuelo, or scarf, and sash around his waist. In the morning encierro he always wears a red, green and white sweatshirt given to him by an American priest who he met in Pamplona the day before his first run in 1987.

Though Tom Turley's exploits may seem romantic to some young Americans and tempt them to travel to Pamplona to run with the bulls as Tom does, they should all know that the encierro is not all about romance and adventure. Running with the bulls is also very much about death.

ON July 13, 1995, a 22-year-old American died on the horns. Matthew Peter Tassio of Glen Ellyn, Illinois had been in Fiesta one day when the long, sharp horn of a fighting bull pierced his aorta. He died almost instantly in the plaza fronting the town hall. It was then and remains the saddest event in the history of the American experience. This was the first death of an American in the encierro. Eight years later people still talk about Matthew Tassio, almost as if they knew him. A softer layer of the deep sadness that will never leave his family and friends still exists in Pamplona and will probably always exist.

Many things about fiesta are overstated, over romanticized, but this young man really was the all-American youth. Finished with college, a job awaiting him at Motorola upon his return from the continent, he had charged across Europe that summer in a carefree way like thousands of his peers, making his way into Pamplona on 12 July when fiesta was already in full swing. In the truest sense of the phrase, Matthew was one of the true stars of the American experience, one of the young ones mentioned earlier - the thousands of university students who wander the cobblestones day and night, giving themselves over fully to the masquerade.

Any English-speaker who wants to learn about running with bulls can glean valuable information at Bar Txoko on Plaza del Castillo each morning, a place where experienced runners gather after the run. Over a drink with one of these colorful characters you can learn a lot about this unique ritual. Sadly, Matthew Peter Tassio never had the chance to have that drink.

In the thirty seconds he was in the encierro he only had the chance to do two things. In both instances he innocently and unknowingly violated cardinal rules of bullrunning, doing things he would have strongly been advised to avoid by any experienced runner. As the bulls approached his position at the town hall he chose to run across the course in a jaywalking fashion rather than running with the flow toward the bullring. Predictably his movement across the course caused him to bump into another runner and both of them fell to the ground. Once Tassio was down on the street in the path of the oncoming herd he made the fatal mistake of responding to his natural instinct, the exact same instinct all of us have when we fall to the ground - he tried to get up, struggled to return to his feet.

Had Tassio not run across the course or had he stayed motionless on the ground after being knocked down to the street, the odds are great that he would have lived to have that drink at Bar Txoko. A fighting bull is a great athlete. A bull will do everything in its considerable power to avoid stepping on anything that appears to be an uneven surface, for to do so may throw it off balance. Each morning bulls step over and around many who have been knocked down or fallen in their path. Occasionally the entire herd hurdles a fallen runner without leaving so much as a hoofprint on his back. Had Tassio remained still, motionless in the street, as an experienced runner would have done in that situation, the strong likelihood is he would have emerged unscathed.

This handsome, vibrant young American was killed in the very prime of his life by the kind of bull the Spanish refer to as noble. This was not a bad-tempered animal intent on attacking or inflicting injury. In fact, the authorities judged this bull, named Castellano, the best of the 48 bulls that appeared in the bullring that Fiesta. That morning Castellano broke from the corral in first position, ahead of the steers, and he gained speed as he traveled up the steep incline of Santo Domingo, all the time running out front. In fact, following his encounter with Matthew, he led the herd through the whole half-mile course to the bullring without another incident. When the bull encountered Tassio, the animal was just clearing its path. And but for that brief moment, Castellano's run was clean.

There have been instances in Pamplona where bulls have savagely and repeatedly attacked runners, mauling them. The most famous incident is one sometimes referred to as "the Riley roll around" that happened on July 12, 1988 when two extraordinary runners, twin brothers from California, were among a large number who rode in ambulances. The bulls that injured the Rileys and others had become separated from the herd. All along the course, from the corral to the bullring, the bulls individually set up shop and got down to the business of dominating and attacking anything that moved in their line of sight. This was not the case on the morning the young American died.

When Tassio started to get up he was directly in Castellano's line of vision. A bull's eyes are usually downcast when they are running. They are watching the terrain. Tassio had to have appeared as a threat, nuisance or obstacle to Castellano. The bull, with its tremendous power and speed, hardly slowed. As Castellano barreled by, he tossed his head and hooked, attempting to clear his path of an obvious obstruction. Tassio was off the horn as quickly as he was on it. It was but an instant. The young man demonstrated strong character, a strong will to live, as he stood up one last time. He died moments later.

The Spanish understand death differently and better than we do in American culture. Death is treated with dignity and respect, then life, or fiesta in this instance, resumes all the more intensely. They have a saying that at the time of a death that we all should embrace ourselves, those we love, and life itself all the tighter. That is what happened that day in Pamplona.

In the afternoon all of Pamplona honored the young American who had come into Fiesta the day before. Before the bullfight there was a moment of silence in the Plaza de Toros followed by a band playing the traditional anthem for a fallen soldier. When the time came for Matador Juan Mora to face Castellano, the matador raised his montera or hat to the sky, signaling his dedication of the bullfight to the soul of this youth who danced across the cobblestones of Pamplona ever so briefly one night and died in the early morning light of the following day.

The bull fought bravely and Mora triumphed with Castellano. During the matador's tour of the ring following the death of Castellano, the senior American bullrunner, Joe Distler, stepped into the bullring to thank Mora on behalf of all Americans for his gesture. A picture of the American bullrunner and the matador embracing ran full page around Spain.

Late that night an impromptu, informal memorial service took place as young people from around the world created a makeshift monument on the spot where Matthew Tassio was killed. They set candles on the cobblestone street and piled up scarves, sashes, sweatshirts with university logos, flags, baseball caps, T-shirts and an assortment of curious things like a toy saxophone. At times they sang songs all of them knew, singing softly to guitar accompaniment.

The next day the entire city responded emotionally when Tassio's youthful parents arrived in Pamplona. Many wanted to approach them. Few knew what to say. Few would know what to say today. That Matthew Peter Tassio did not get to do all the things he wanted to do in life, that he was unable to fulfill the great promise within him is terribly tragic. The young runner was honored by the Rev. Miguel Flamarique at a mass in the chapel of San Fermín in the great San Lorenzo church on July 14, the final day of Fiesta.

Matthew Peter Tassio will never be forgotten by anyone who was in Pamplona that year. The hope will always be that nothing like this will happen again. If any young American reads this and realizes how quickly an athletic young countryman can die in the encierro and refrains from entering the run for that reason, or postpones running in the encierro until he or she has had a long conversation with one who knows the encierro well, then in a small way Michael Peter Tassio will continue to live in Pamplona through them. Though they never knew their countryman, when they dance on the cobblestones, they will dance for him.

Foreigners of all nations have been paying the price for running bulls for years. Prior to Tassio's death the worst goring of an American in Pamplona was inflicted on a young military man named Townsend who took the horn more than once in front of Café Flores on Estafeta. He lost great amounts of blood, and many believe his great physical condition saved his life.

An equally severe injury was suffered by Robin Kelley O'Connor in the Navarran town of Sanguesa in 1982. O'Connor was pinned against a wall by a toro bravo and the horn went straight through his gut, entering just below the navel and exiting through his back. The injury required three surgeries over a month. A sidebar to the O'Connor goring is that the injury caused him to miss his flight home the following day, a Madrid-Malaga-New York flight that crashed at the end of the Malaga runway killing most and severely burning survivors. Being gored saved his life. The recovery took months. He has returned to the encierro at times and his brother

Robin Kelley O'Connor downed and then run through by the horn of a bull in Sanguessa, Spain on September 12, 1982.

Steve continues to run bulls. In fact, it seems the rule among many foreign runners, those who are injured and those close to them, shrug off the incidents and return to the street when their wounds heal.

The foreign crowd has had its own in-house physician for over 40 years in Frank McGuinness, M.D., a lovable man known as "Dr. Frank." He too was gored when he was trapped in one of the worst montons in the history of the encierro. A montón, or mountain, happens in the encierro when runners fall and others pile on top of them, creating a mass of humanity too tall for the bulls to hurdle.

Left to right: Fiesta regulars Robin Kelley O'Connor, Joe Distler, Tom Gowen, Jesse Graham and the man known as "Bomber." Jose Antonio Sanz Amador, a wonderful friend to many foreigners, a fine bullrunner and an extraordinary magician kneels in the foreground.

The animals slam into the mass and become tangled with the runners. Though this has happened in the streets of the route, it is more likely to occur in the tunnel leading to the bullring, the place where McGuinness was caught. When the bulls broke free and went onto the sand, people scrambled to save themselves and ran away. Frank stayed. He accompanied the medical team to the enfermeria or medical center in the bullring and assisted Pamplona physicians for a long time as they unsuccessfully tried to revive a young Spanish runner. Only when that work was finished did Frank mention that his injuries required stitches.

W HEN Pamplona gets into an American's blood, it seems it never leaves. In 1949 a young American named Harry Connick Sr. was working in Casablanca, Morocco, and fell in love with bullfighting.

He befriended Antonio Bienvenida, a well-known Spanish matador. He lent the torero his Studebaker, which the bullfighter loved, and the two struck a bargain in which the matador agreed to train Harry to become a bullfighter. As Connick made preparations to move to the ranch he contracted tuberculosis, forcing him to return to the states for a long hospitalization. Connick, the father of his famous namesake singer-songwriter-actor, went on to hold what is arguably the most powerful elected political position in the most political state in the nation, District Attorney of New Orleans. He has now served as D.A. for 30 years, and he also fronts his own big band, playing weekly locally and on occasion traveling to far-away gigs. One would have thought the prosecutor/crooner might have forgotten all about the bulls over 49 years, but the bug that bit him in his youth created an itch he could not scratch. In 1998 Connick finally came into Fiesta with his wife Alonda. He was in his early seventies when he ran with the Miura bulls in Santo Domingo. The next year D.A. Connick could have convened court in Plaza del Castillo as he was in the company of Judge Camille Buras and her husband, lawyer Mike Tifft, as well as Defense Counsel Bill Wessel and his wife Cissie.

COLLECTION OF HARRY CONNICK SR.

Harry Connick with the author in 1998, moments after having run the Miura bulls. Mouton sports a cast from a broken arm suffered in a fall on opening day at the entrance to the bullring. His injury, like many others, was caused by a runner, not a bull.

American artist Warren Parker lives
abroad much of the year and makes
Pamplona an annual destination.

Warren Parker, Vic Labat, and Don Barry are a colorful crew. Other than their friendship which causes them to share lodging in Pamplona, there is not much commonality among them. Barry, a professor of European history for nearly thirty years has the long view of fiesta and can envision it as it was centuries ago. Labat, a businessman with interests in Africa and the United States, uses the other side of his brain and makes sketches of Pamplona's fiesta. Parker runs bulls and holds court in the back bar of his favorite haunt on the main square. His taurine paintings and monoprints have been exhibited in France and Spain.

In July of 1959 when Hemingway was seeing Pamplona for the last time, Bob Jones was seeing it for the first time. Jones continues to return to fiesta all these years later. As a toddler he took his first steps in the Louisiana governor's mansion during his father's term as Governor and he later served in both houses of the state legislature and made a run for Governor himself.

He wrote to his mom and dad from Pamplona and forty-three years later his letter offers proof that neither

Bob Jones in Pamplona, 1959.

160

Part of a contingent that calls themselves the "Ragin' Cajun Runners:" Bob Jones at left with Billy Blakeman and David Jones sitting on a barricade in front of town hall before the encierro.

the celebration nor its impact on young Americans has changed much in the modern era. Describing his arrival in Pamplona with the celebration underway, Jones mentions the "confusion and noise" being "just like the French Quarter during Mardi Gras." He wrote that he was sure he "could write a book on Pamplona," a thought many Americans have had over the years. Bob Jones never wrote that book, but more than four decades later he published this one. By the time his first fiesta experience was ending, Jones was no longer comparing Fiesta to Mardi Gras; he was saying you would have "to multiply Mardi Gras by at least three times and jam it into a city a quarter the size of New Orleans."

He was hooked on travel and thrill-seeking adventure in his youth and since then he and his wife, Sarah, as well as their children, Houston, Gambrelle, Quinn and Jennifer have traveled widely and had experiences that have extended to climbing Mt. Kilimanjaro twice, working hands-on at an archeological dig at Ain Ghazal in Jordan, attending Carnival in Rio, and attending ballet and opera performances at La Scala, Garnier, and the Met. In 2001 he achieved a tough goal when he hit a target that moves every year with the publication of the Michelin restaurant guidebook. At the end of that May he had dined in every three star restaurant listed in France. Though he has roamed far and wide since 1959, he has found nothing that replicates the feelings provided by the encierro and Sanfermines.

Charlie Cole

Pamplona has a strange effect on a lot of people. Charlie and Kathy Cole originally came to Fiesta for only a day or two, in the same way they might visit any other well-known attraction or event. Before the first day of Sanfermines had ended for the Coles they were talking to the hotel about reservations for the following year, and like so many before them they have become regulars.

THE AMERICANS have risk takers and spectators among them. The best example of the former group was probably provided by the twin Riley brothers, Jim and John. They ran la curva as well as it has ever been run, but maybe more dangerously than it needed to be run. Their detractors said their style was too dominating, that they were in the bulls' space, forcing the bulls to do things because of their presence.

That they were brave is beyond dispute; that they took too many risks is arguable. It is true that most mornings Jim Riley's run ended when a bull hit him with the flat of its horn and tossed him to the wall. One of the greatest runners who ever lived, Matt Carney, expressed the opinion that they were among the best of the bunch of foreigners and toward the end of his life Carney stood at the curve, several yards from where the Rileys were running, in a front-row seat of sorts for their daily heart-stopping show.

Hal Jennings, another Californian who penned a Pamplona novel titled *Cowards Of Us All*, was one of the most exciting runners to watch during the late eighties. He is a superb athlete and his ath-leticism allowed him to do things among the throngs of runners that others would never be capable of. Like a great running back Jennings did amazing things to negotiate his way to the most dan-gerous place in the street and hold that place all the way into the bullring. One could watch video replays of Jennings' runs over and over and never believe what he had done. He took monumental risks, incurred injuries, broke bones and put his life on the line.

The Rileys stopped coming to Pamplona after the day they both sustained serious injuries and John had to pull a bull off Jim as he was being mauled in the middle of Estafeta directly beneath the balcony where both Riley wives and their children were watching. Jennings also stopped coming suddenly. With their departures a controversial era for foreigners in the street ended, for today people still argue whether those three men were great bullrunners or sim-ply great daredevils.

Twins Jim and John Riley became well known in the 1980s for their exploits in the encierro. In the beginning they ran the top of Estafeta into the bullring. Though they often started at different points on opposite sides of the street, many photos show them ending up side by side on the horns. They are mirror twins and as unbelievable as it sounds, the left-handed brother was usually on the right horn with his right-handed counterpart on the left horn. By the end of the decade, the brothers ran la curva together. On the fateful morning of the now-infamous Riley roll-around – July 12, 1988 – one of the worst encierros of the modern era in terms of injuries – the following sequence of events occurred as depicted in the numbered photographs.

1. John Riley, in red shirt and red headband, dashes into Estafeta on the horns of two bulls.

2. A bull slips in the curve, becomes disoriented, and charges a doorway, goring a man in blue. Jim Riley, in whites with a red stripe across his shirt and long sleeves, moves toward the bull to lure it from the doorway.

3. Jim, with one foot on the sidewalk, newspaper pointed toward the bull, attempts to keep the animal's attention as it looks away.

4. As Jim slips, the bull attacks.

5. The bull hooks a horn under Jim's leg.

6. With great force the bull tosses Jim to the center of the street where he lands directly on his head.

7. The bull continues to lift Jim off the cobblestones and pound him to the ground.

8. Two runners close in and attempt to lure the suelto away from Jim; Riley's body is almost completely obscured by the figure of the bull on top of him.

9. John Riley runs back down the street, sensing his brother's peril, to find him pinned beneath the bull. John grabs the bull by its horn and begins to punch it in the nose.

10. As the bull focuses on John, Jim scrambles away on all fours.

11. John Riley leads the bull away from his brother and toward the bullring. The bull then pushed John aside, tossing him into the wall and separating his shoulder. Jim suffered multiple orthopedic injuries.

Two close friends, John Asta and Debbie Reppenhagen, also number among the large crowd that skis the toughest slopes, flies off the sides of mountains, bungee jumps and signs up for almost any available activity that provides an adrenalin rush and risk. Asta also had a comedic side and he once ran the bulls dressed as an Arab sheik, another time in a gorilla suit. Though Reppenhagen still flies off mountains, still runs bulls in Pamplona, and continues to live as an expatriate in Europe, John is no longer among those in her crowd. Asta died on the Matterhorn during a Thanksgiving trip when he skied into a crevasse. He was skiing out of bounds at the time. John Asta lived and died out of bounds.

Some bullrunners have retired to become avid spectators. This is a more contemplative lot and this is where most of the writers are.

Author Allen Josephs, a 40-year veteran of summers in Spain, is a noted authority on Hemingway, Spanish literature and bullfighting.

First among both groups is Allen Josephs who first went to Spain 40 years ago, befriended Matador John Fulton and came to know almost every American who ever seriously followed the bulls from feria to feria. An acknowledged expert on bullfighting and Spain, Josephs served as president of The Ernest Hemingway Foundation and Society from 1996 to 1999 and he has written an in-depth book on bullfighting titled *Ritual and Sacrifice in The Corrida: The Saga of César Rincón*. Before that he published *White Wall of Spain: The Mysteries of Andalusian Culture*; *For Whom The Bell Tolls: Ernest Hemingway's*

166

Jesse Graham in trademark vest.

Undiscovered Country; *Only Mystery: Federico Garcia Lorca's poetry in Word and Image;* and other works, some of which have been published in Spain.

    Among the risk takers and spectators there are also those who defy categorization, men who are both active and reflective, full out participants as well as chroniclers of the history of the American experience in Pamplona. Jesse Graham, a citizen of the U.S. and Great Britain, has spent 30 years or more running the bulls and living Fiesta. At home in Los Angeles he is a talented screenwriter who has also written short pieces about Pamplona. It is Graham who is the greatest repository of the history of the foreign experience in the modern era. He has lived it and kept a record of it, and is like a human vault. A close friend of Graham's, Tom Gowen, similarly lives it all every July, running the bulls and bars. And in the months following Fiesta, Tom writes poems, some having distinct Fiesta themes.

THE AMERICAN crowd also includes several acknowledged experts on the corrida. Tom Weitzner saw his first bullfight in Marseille,

GERRY DAWES

Two of the boys of summer, George Danick, the one called "Australian George" and Tom Gowen, in the bullring following an afternoon sitting in the peña section of the plaza.

France in 1948 in the pouring rain and was so moved by the potential that was present, though nothing materialized in the deluge that day, that a large part of his life became devoted to his love of this art. He has spent 50-plus years following the bulls during Spain's six-month season and he has traveled the South American circuit some winter seasons.

As a teenager and college student Bill Lyon rambled around Spain, a place where he found everything he wanted in life. Upon graduation from Yale 40 years ago Bill settled in Spain to stay, becoming a respected authority on la fiesta brava or the bullfight. He is the only American to ever have worked as chief critic for a major Spanish newspaper, and in his time he has published reviews and articles in many Spanish papers and periodicals. Lyon still lives in Madrid as does his only son, Santiago Lyon, chief of photography for the Associated Press in Spain. It has not been all bullfighting for these two for when Santi was a child he and his dad took bicycle trips in the countryside, covering a different province each year.

No taurine expert's story is more unlikely than that of a young girl from Brooklyn named Muriel Feiner. Thirty years ago she came to Spain to improve her Spanish, fell in love with bullfighting and a bullfighter. In Madrid she tried to join taurine clubs but at that time, in that macho culture, the little gringo girl was turned away. Undaunted, Feiner founded Club Internacional Taurino and though she was the only member she proudly presented her credentials to gain admittance to apartados and other events. Over the years and the course of her writing numerous articles in Spanish on the subject she has erased the original prejudice she encountered. She has published two well-received volumes: *La Mujer En El Mundo Del Toro* and *Los Protagonistas De La Fiesta*. The English translation of her book *Women In Bullfighting* is now slated for U.S. publication. She married her Bullfighter, Matador Pedro Giraldo, when he was still a novillero, and they live in Madrid with their children, Pedro and Blanca Veronica.

No mention of foreign experts on bullfighting would be complete without a mention of Michael Wigram, an Englishman who lives in Madrid. Wigram sees more corridas in a season than the most active matador, and his understanding and knowledge of the history of this art form is encyclopedic. Though many disagree with some of the things he writes and some believe Wigram likes argument for argument's sake, or as the Spanish say, likes to put the devil's tail in the soup, his annual essays at the end of the bullfighting season are reason enough to subscribe to the publications of either the London or New York Taurino Clubs who publish them.

Every circus has its ringleaders, master of ceremonies and its clowns. This circus operates without a ringleader or any ceremony, but it has had an endearing clown for over forty years, Dave Pierce. He is a brilliant man, a Canadian who has lived in Paris for many years. Built like an NBA basketball player, if not as heavy, this novelist-songwriter, world-class raconteur and bon vivant has been the life of the party, sometimes the whole party, for a long time. Big

GERRY DAWES

Big Dave Pierce strolls to the bullring with Lore Monnig, President of Club Taurino New York. Lore actually looks pretty, while Dave looks ridiculous by design. On days when Big Dave dressed as a matador, he always wore a watch that was set two hours off to insure he would miss his appointment with destiny. This is everyday attire for Pierce.

Dave Pierce as he is known, has a tailor in Paris doll him up in some of the most outrageous outfits seen anywhere. He even has a matador's suit which he has worn to the Pamplona plaza. For anyone else Dave's wardrobe would be costumes. For David the outfits are everyday apparel.

Pierce's obvious heir apparent is Mark Oldfield who is part of a triumvirate of adopted Americans who head a crew known collectively as "The Sheffields." They are a rolling riot headed by Paul Bower, Mark Oldfield and Chris Williams. Two are pretty much cockney blokes while the other is something of a blueblood. It takes all of thirty seconds to figure out who's who. There are no others among foreigners quite like these fellows. They know everything there is to know about Fiesta and the Basque country, especially in their respective areas of expertise: alcohol consumption and eating. What they don't know, they make up. They have often danced the Dianas at dawn on successive days without having had any sleep. No one matches their pace in Pamplona and few would want to try.

Despite its macho image, the American experience has not been and is not all about guys. In fact, among young backpackers the girls seem to outnumber boys. Among Americans who attend regularly, there are probably nearly as many women as men. Of the many, a few will be mentioned here to illustrate their diverse interests and backgrounds.

Few men could keep pace with Lore Monnig, President of New York Club Taurino, who once saw 158 bullfights in a season. With her high energy she moves in a blur. By contrast, many have waited on the slow-moving southern belle from Georgia, Nancy Fortier, for it takes her longer to dress than it does a matador. Monnig has contributed a lot through the taurine club, and Fortier's presence and humor complement that of her longtime companion, Noel Chandler. One of Fortier's contributions to fiesta was Harriet McGinty Mitchell, another Atlanta beauty. Both Nancy and Harriet are always beautifully dressed, but far more impressive is the secret they have shared with no one – how both of them always appear well-rested in a town where no one sleeps. Fortier, Mitchell and Monnig have a far greater interest in and deeper understanding of bullfighting than many men in the foreign contingent.

A pair of ladies who go back longer than half of the American cuadrilla are Junerose Conlin and her close friend Caroline McIntyre. Junerose was a natural for fiesta from her first day in Plaza del Castillo and for several years was linked with a Navarran matador and spent summers going to corridas and bull ranches. Junerose has lived in Spain for stretches of time, teaching young children. Caroline was a high-powered corporate executive who dropped out and sought serenity by moving to an island where she became a yoga teacher. This strict vegetarian revels in an atmosphere where animals are killed every afternoon and serenity is something that exists way beyond the city limits.

Few women have as much knowledge about the American experience as Carol Leimroth, co-author of *Peak Experience*, a rare book examining this phenomenon of seekers in Sanfermines. Leimroth was the last love of Matt Carney, the figure most responsible for there being a continuum of the American experience in the modern era. She shared his life in France, Ireland and Spain. Unlike her close friends, Judy Nadelson and Esti Marpet, who are in Pamplona every year, Carol has chosen not to return since the Mass honoring and memorializing Carney in 1989. A lot of the crowd goes through Paris every summer to dine with her and many call her Moms, an endearing term reflective of the role she has played in so many lives.

A younger generation of women continue this legacy. Lisa Fitch Stefanski, first appeared in Pamplona at age 17, fell in love with the country and moved to Spain shortly thereafter to study the language and work in equestrian centers. She has returned a number of times and now thinks about the day when her baby, Alexandra, will be old enough to dance behind a peña band. Contemporaries of Lisa – Laura, Anna and Maricarmen Josephs, Spanish speakers since their youth, are as much at home in Pamplona as they are in their father Allen Josephs' home in Pensacola, Florida. Maricarmen and Laura are almost always in fiesta, and Anna often joins them.

A young beauty recently returned to Fiesta after an absence of 10 or more years. She is an American though she was reared and schooled in Ireland and Paris. Deirdre Carney, the daughter of Carol Leimroth and the late Matt Carney, is a young woman blessed with her parents' gracious charm and confidence. While in Fiesta her godfather, Noel Chandler, looked after her, putting her up in the Matt Carney suite of his Pamplona home. In the after-

COLLECTION OF NOEL CHANDLER

Deirdre Carney stands on the right side of her godfather, Noel Chandler, who is flanked by Deirdre's Parisian friend, Denise.

noons she sat near Chandler in the bullring in the seat her father occupied for many years.

THE ranks of Americans in Fiesta have included famous artists, writers, newsmen, actors and celebrities: Orson Welles, Ava Gardner, Arthur Miller, Robert Trout, James Michener, Art Buchwald, Irwin Shaw, Daryl Zanuck, George Plimpton, James Jones and Swifty Lazar. Some brought larger than life personas with them, but Pamplona is a larger than life experience and it is not impressed by famous names. No one talks about them any longer. Few remember any of them. But there are some who will never be forgotten though they have passed on, people others still talk about constantly in the present tense as if they were about to walk around the corner and join them for a drink. They are more than remembered.

To be remembered in Fiesta at all one must possess the prominent accomplishments and imposing presence of a Matt Carney, John Fulton, Joe Distler or Alice Hall. Fulton was well known in both the world of bullfighting and art. His death garnered a huge obituary in *The New York Times* of the kind normally reserved for heads of state. Like John Fulton, Matt Carney and Alice Hall are no longer with us but their stories remain and some will be retold here for they are hallmarks in Hemingway's legacy.

A true trace of the continuum of the American experience in Fiesta follows a straight line through the lives of three men. Ernest Hemingway described the experience; Matt Carney defined it; and Joe Distler continues to live it. Each of them have had their own eras which together cover the period from 1923 to 2002. These

Joe Distler running full out on the horns in Estafeta. This is the way Navarrans run, the way Carney ran, how Distler runs, and a way few others dare to run.

three dominate the foreground of the American experience while two very different people illuminate the background: Matador John Fulton achieved more than any American in bullfighting; Alice Hall saw more bullfights in more seasons and knew more about them than any American aficionada of her time.

Distler is the most prominent American in Fiesta today, having run with the bulls in the encierro every day for 34 years, over 300 times. Many Americans experience Fiesta in their youth, promising themselves and everyone in earshot that they will return each year only to fade from the scene forever following the final ceremony. Joe never broke the youthful promise he made to himself, to others and to Spain. And incredibly, Distler has never missed an appointment with the toros.

Even now in his fifties he can be seen every morning negotiating the most dangerous part of the encierro, la curva. As he races into Estafeta on the horns, it is as if time has stood still for him. It is not likely that any American will ever match his record for consecutive encierros in Pamplona.

When Distler first landed in Fiesta he was young, handsome and dashing, penniless and clueless, but not without talent. His gifts would eventually take him through a life of acting, modeling, writing, owning a restaurant, teaching English literature and living as an adventurer whose travels have extended through China, Africa, Israel, Mexico, Turkey, South America and India. As the millennium tolled, Distler was hosting a New Year's Eve party in the Hemingway suite of Hotel La Perla in Pamplona, a town that is as much his home as Paris and New York. He owns an apartment just off Plaza del Castillo, a house on the Mediterranean near Alicante, has a place in Paris and another in Greenwich Village. He knows all of those places well and divides his time among them, though like Hemingway before him he likes Spain best of all.

Of all the gifts Distler has received in Fiesta one of the greatest was his friendship with Carney, a man who made an indelible mark on Fiesta on both the Spanish and American sides and was well established in Pamplona long before Distler came to town.

Matt Carney with author in Plaza del Castillo.

THOUGH Hemingway wrote his novel in the twenties, the American experience in Fiesta was really born in 1950 when several other Americans trooped into Fiesta. David Black, Hal Casteel, Cliff Fish, Jimmy MacPharren, Tom Donaldson and Bob Kopp continued in real life what Hemingway's fiction had begun. They arrived in Pamplona nearly twenty years after Hemingway's last appearance in Fiesta in 1931 and a year later they were joined by Matt Carney.

Carney's glory days extended to the late eighties but when he first arrived in Pamplona at the dawning of the fifties the political world was changing and everything seemed possible to those who had fought the bloody battles and won the big war. With this spirit Matt joined a small band of expatriates for what he would call a lark with the bulls. In those days Carney lived in Paris. A veteran of the Pacific campaign, Matt was another young writer seeking inspiration in the City of Light. He was a scholar of philosophy and literature and he passionately continued those pursuits until his death. Over time, Carney's Irish-American good looks made him one of the premier male models on the continent and with that work came enough money to buy three homes in Europe.

His life was enviable, a life of dreams for the young Americans

176

who would read about him in James Michener's *Iberia*. The charismatic Carney was a magnet in Pamplona. For a young romantic, being in Matt's presence was like seeing the incarnation of one's own dream. He was the dashing, handsome, brilliant, brave man loose on the continent. But his legend lives not because of his lifestyle, looks, writing or charisma, but because of his exploits in the encierro, the running of the bulls.

What was it that Carney did and why does his spirit live?

Photographs tell the story in part. There are hundreds of pic-

Legends one and all. Matt Carney, Nancy Fortier, Noel Chandler, Bruce Clark and Carol Leimroth captured at an apartado in Pamplona by the most famous bullfight photographer in history, Paco Cano.

tures of him running in the encierro, a lovely grin spreading across his face, displaying the demeanor of a gentleman on a Sunday stroll in a peaceful park, all the while racing up the street on the horns, dancing with destiny and death.

The encierro unfolds quickly and is measured in seconds. There is madness and in the midst of that madness, all the way until his death, Carney was always a portrait of composure, serenity and joy. He talked about the metaphysics of the encierro. He said, "When the bulls are close you pick them up and you are with them ... then there is transcendence."

Everyone experiences fear in the encierro. Carney's love of the experience was greater than his fear of it. There are many great Navarran runners, but no foreigner has ever run with more artistry than Carney. He was almost always there, with the herd, in the aura of danger and on the horns. Some oldtimers in Pamplona joke about Carney's uncanny knack for finding his way to and running with the herd in crowded conditions, saying the steers communicated with the bulls in the corral, telling them about the man who would be waiting for them near the bullring. The steers told the bulls to look for the tall, serene one who knew the way through the storm.

To fully comprehend Carney's legend built through bullrunning one must first understand that when he began to participate in the encierro it was something that had belonged exclusively to the Navarrans for hundreds of years, and Carney would be the first to explain to foreigners that bullrunning is truly a Spanish thing, a Navarran thing. On any morning of any Fiesta there are many local runners who run better than any American or other foreigner ever will. Navarrans begin to run bulls when they are boys and they run often in the long days of the late summer months in the pueblos of northern Spain. The young runners almost always run at the side of an older, more experienced runner, a master. The experience, expertise, emotional investment and instinctive feel a Navarran has in the encierro cannot truly be matched or rivaled by those from other cultures. But phenomenal local runners in Pamplona gave Carney his greatest accolade when they said over and over, "Matt Carney runs like a Navarran."

Matt Carney rests his hand on the shoulder of an old friend, Antanasio, and smiles as the two of them chat like fellows strolling in a park while the herd closes in. It was hundreds of mornings like this that made Matt Carney a legend.

Carney ran the bulls the way he danced and sang, the way he did everything, with great joy. What Carney did in the encierro was art and it evoked emotion. He was quick to tell anyone that for all the bluster they might hear in the cafés of Pamplona there is only one reason to run with the bulls: for the alegría, the sheer joy of it. "I run the bulls for joy, which is the chief ingredient of generosity," Carney said.

On his last day in Fiesta, in the cool, overcast weather of July 14, 1987, Carney stood near a doorway at the beginning of Estafeta, on the curve of the bullrun, minutes before the rocket. His era was ending and he knew it. No one else did. He had run the bulls for almost 40 years and now, in the streets he loved, his time was short

Best friends Matt Carney and Noel Chandler

and the Fiesta that made him a legend was getting its last glimpse of him. He was 64 years old and he knew that he was dying of cancer, a secret he had shared only with his longtime companion, Carol Leimroth, the great love of his life.

All that Fiesta Carney and I shared an informal early morning ritual; a long, rambling, gentle conversation before walking to the statue of the Saint in Santo Domingo for a more formal ritual. There we offered a prayer for five minutes of grace. We paid our respects to the saint and then stood the bulls near this doorway on the curve, a doorway Americans still refer to as Matt's door. All week he and I stood and watched the bulls rush by, slam into the corner barricade and turn into the long straightaway leading to the ring.

That last morning, an hour before the encierro, I rang the buzzer at Chandler's apartment on Estafeta where Carney lived in Fiesta. We walked to the rear of the flat and stood on a balcony facing the mountains. There we had a drink and looked over the tile rooftops and church spires to the foothills. Carney's face, even when relaxed, was expressive, ruggedly handsome. The whole of his head, including his infectious Irish grin, seemed to have been sculpted to feature eyes that were often fixed in an almost piercing stare before softening to an amused glint. Almost everything he said sounded like dialogue written for a movie matinee idol, the kind he easily could have been, given his looks and charm. He found joy in all things around him. The delight he showed over a small bird landing on a nearby rooftop was the joy of a young child rather than a World War II veteran, a Sorbonne-educated philosopher and writer who was growing old and facing death.

On the balcony before the bullrun we talked about a lot of things, but never about the encierro. Carney had run more encierros than any foreigner in the history of Fiesta and it was not something he needed to talk about, though it occupied the minds of almost everyone else in town at that time of day. Our conversations on those chilly mornings were mostly about his life in Lettermullan, Ireland, about his neighbors there, how unspoiled they were. Though he had a flat in Paris and a country house in the south of France, he always seemed most excited by his small cottage with the thatched roof west of Galway. As a philosopher and writer, Carney thought and wrote about complex matters but seemed most at home in simple settings. The Irish neighbors he talked about seemed to share his most obvious attribute, generosity. "They care about humans in a way damn few do," he said.

He was not running that year. His medical condition was a secret only he and Carol shared though he was at an age when a graceful retirement from the encierro would have been deemed appropriate by everyone. We had stood together for seven straight mornings, watching from a doorway just before la curva, the big bend at the end of Mercaderes.

On that last day, with about a minute remaining before the rocket, Carney grinned, gave me a hug and a pat on the back. He said, "Ah, kid, the alegría." The joy. His eyes shone brighter than usual. In the faint, shadowy light in the corner of the street his face looked younger. All the years were gone. The joy of Fiesta filled him. He touched his heart. He started away from me, toward the bullring.

A runner who was in Estafeta that morning told me that as Carney glided gracefully through the crowd, threading a path in the center of the street moments before the rocket, runners on the sidewalk pointed him out to their friends. He said that in those tense moments when the street feels like a stage poised for combat, Matt was like a great general reviewing his troops, someone to be saluted. Carney's old friends, Spaniards he had run with for years, shouted a word or two to him. No one could miss him. Not those who knew him and recognized him, and not those who only sensed the presence of a real figura, a man who commanded respect earned here on hundreds of mornings like this one.

Nearly 40 years of mornings had passed since Carney first hiked into Pamplona with a G.I. rucksack and entered his first encierro. Today he was going to run with the bulls, Miura bulls, one last time. It was his farewell encierro. He moved up the crowded course in the center of the street. This stretch of the run was very congested. When the rocket fired, bringing bulls into the street, most of the runners scrambled for the sidewalk, trying to get out of harm's way. There were bulls in the center of the street. All his life Matt ran in the center of the street. In the end, when he knew it was the end, he stayed in the center of the street. In the American experience, a remarkable era ended.

Though he was seriously wounded in the encierro in his career, Carney always returned to run again, always in the same elegant and daring style. He will always be remembered as a bull-runner and perhaps a boulevardier, living well in Europe, though life was much more to this man. Bullrunning was only a few days in July and Matt wrote every day of his life. He meant for his literary work to be his legacy. *Peripheral American*, his philosophical memoir, devotes a chapter to his history in Fiesta, his thoughts about Fiesta and the feelings of transcendence he experienced in the encierro. The Fiesta chapter is, however, but one of 29. This ratio of 1:29 reflects the importance Carney placed upon his accomplishments as a bullrunner in contrast to the much greater emphasis he placed upon his work as a writer and philosopher.

Unfortunately, as hard as he worked as a writer, the critical accept-ance, commercial success and popular approval that Hemingway enjoyed eluded Carney entirely.

As he was dying he continued to write every day in his cottage along the rocky shore where the Bay of Galway meets the Atlantic Ocean. He accepted his fate with the same courage he exhibited in the encierro. At peace, he chose to die in his home in Ireland. On Christmas Eve 1988, Matt Carney died and on the 27th of December, the 66th anniversary of his birth, he was buried in the front garden of Connemara cottage in a grave high above the sea, marked by a large cross inscribed with the epitaph *"Here Lies A Celtic Warrior."*

Close friends made the journey to Ireland toward the end. The winter rain beat cold on the cottage. Indoors Matt sat by the fire. To old friends in Ireland he was Matthew, and they would remember his kindness, the neighborly things he did and his formidable talent for carving walking sticks. Far away in Pamplona he would be remembered for other things. The 1989 Fiesta program carried a Carney letter of *adiós* to Pamplona. The poetic letter, written on his deathbed in Ireland, had generosity as its theme.

THE BEGINNING of all this, of course, was with the man that put Pamplona on the world map. He founded the legacy, left a testament interpreted in thousands of ways by the heirs and legatees. First there was Ernest Hemingway and last there will be Ernest Hemingway. It will always be Hemingway and for very good cause. No other American writer has loved Spain, Fiesta and bullfighting more than Hemingway, and it is not likely that any other American writer will ever make such an imprint on the consciousness of this proud foreign culture. A young Ernest Hemingway first fell in love with Fiesta in the twenties and his loyalty to Fiesta would last until his death in 1961, longer than any other love of his life. After the pub-lication of *The Sun Also Rises*, titled *Fiesta* in Spain, Hemingway was vaulted into fame and neither he nor Fiesta would ever be the same.

The author also wrote about characters and events in the

Ernest Hemingway flanked by Cayetano Ordóñez, the model for Matador Pedro Romero in The Sun Also Rises, *and Cayetano's son, the incomparable Matador Antonio Ordóñez.*

taurine world in *Death In The Afternoon*, an acclaimed book about bullfighting. His final work on the subject, *The Dangerous Summer*, was originally a long article for *Life* magazine chronicling a season of corridas shared by two rival toreros, the elegant Luis Miguel Dominguin and the incomparable Antonio Ordóñez, the son of matador Cayetano Ordóñez who was the model for Pedro Romero, the fictional torero in *The Sun Also Rises*.

Hemingway's last summer in Spain, 1959, he traveled to fiesta in the company of Matador Antonio Ordóñez. Ordóñez was not appearing on a cartel that year and the plan was to party in Pamplona. It had been over thirty-four years since Hemingway had seen Antonio's father fight bulls in Pamplona, but chronologically Ernest Hemingway was not yet an old man. Nevertheless, he was nearing the end of his life, was old beyond his years, having been banged up in war and air crashes and having lived life full out for too long. He would be dead within two years.

That last fiesta with this friend he deeply admired, the son of a matador who once inspired him, had to have been like the closing of a circle in his life. Pamplona, like Paris, was a place where Hemingway was once young. When Hemingway first saw Spain he had survived war, lived as an expatriate and married, but he was still unformed as an artist, searching for a story for his first novel. In Pamplona Hemingway found the story for his novel and Fiesta also gave birth to his intense lifelong interest in all things Spanish.

As a young man he developed a passion for the corrida and he wrote well about it when he was young. In the summer of 1959, he was writing about bullfighting again, but by that time in his life his talent was sometimes as erratic as his behavior. His behavior was becoming a problem for himself and those around him. He was nearing the end. In 1961, two years after his last Fiesta, Hemingway was buried in Ketchum, Idaho. A front page story in *The New York Times* reported that Hemingway was laid to rest on July 6, the same day that Pamplona begins its riotous celebration of life. The writer's lengthy obituary in *Time* magazine ran eight days later, on the final day of Fiesta that year, July 14. That his final rites would coincide with the beginning of Fiesta, that he was solemnly laid to rest on a hill in Idaho as Plaza del Castillo was filled with revelers, seems somehow fitting.

Though Hemingway's grave and headstone lie in Idaho, a monument to his life exists an ocean away. In this sense Hemingway has never left Spain. A huge bust of the author stands near the entrance to the Pamplona bullring on Paseo Hemingway. It is the only statue at Pamplona's bullring.

American novelist Donny Spicehandler admired the literary giant, and when the Hemingway statue was dedicated in 1968 Spicehandler decorated it with a pañuelo, the red neckerchief symbolic of the celebration. For years thereafter Spicehandler always hung a pañuelo on the statue on opening day. One year he arrived at the statue to find that others had taken over the tradition of dressing Papa for Fiesta, a tribute which continued for many years. Today, as often as not, the statue is not adorned, perhaps a comment on the relevance of Hemingway to younger generations. But there remain some like Charlie Cole who remove their sash and tie it like a scarf around Papa's neck to make sure he is properly attired.

As enthusiastic as Hemingway was about Fiesta, and after attending through the twenties, he all but stopped attending after 1931. He did not revisit Pamplona until 1953. The Spanish Civil War and World War II intervened with the civil war suspending Fiesta and the big war

Ernest Hemingway in 1959, the year of his last visit to Pamplona.

making travel impossible for foreigners. When Fiesta resumed following the civil war and WWII ended, Hemingway did not want to return to a country governed by General Francisco Franco. He had eloquently opposed the general's rise to power and was concerned there might be some repercussions to his actions.

A LOT of time has passed since Hemingway entered Fiesta in 1923. He had his war in Europe, Carney had his war in the Pacific and both were representative of their generation. Joe Distler had no thoughts of being representative of his generation when he arrived in Pamplona. But the world was changing as much as it had during the World Wars. Joe walked into Plaza del Castillo the first time just before the Chicago riots, during the days when the anarchy of Haight-Ashbury was replacing the frivolity of Carnaby Street as a symbol of his generation's values.

When Joe was young he was the true enfant terrible of the American crowd. He is still thought of in that way by some, those who have had feuds with him, real or imagined. His flamboyant and fiery character makes him a heat-seeking missile in the American community at Fiesta, and at times controversy and conflict still swirl about him. But the controversy which occasionally surrounds him contrasts markedly with his unbounded generosity to his friends. His Greenwich Village residence, Spanish homes and bars in New York have been a home away from home for many in the Pamplona crowd. A low-tech or no-tech person who refuses to be introduced to the computer, he is a prolific private correspondent, writing hundreds of let-ters a year to friends. He also regularly vents his strong personal opinions to newspapers in letters to the editor in both New York and Pamplona.

If Carney's charisma was like that of Douglas Fairbanks, a matinee idol of his generation, then Joe Distler's essence is more the stuff of James Dean. In Distler one senses many of the same conflicts that one sensed in Dean. Joe can be very moody, distant and detached. He is both a loner and a gregarious mixer. He is shy and a showoff. He was born a polished performer and he can also quickly affect

Joe Distler

Joe Distler and Matt Carney running side by side in the center of the street with the whole herd steps off of their pace, a scene that played out on many mornings.

the rough and tumble mannerisms of the streetwise kid from Brooklyn.

Matt called him kid, but Joe is no longer a kid, and over 34 years have passed since he first stumbled into the bull run and tried to figure out what he was supposed to do. He has since figured it out pretty well. He has run as well as anyone of any nationality in the encierro. He used to run into the bullring, and though he is older he has moved to the most difficult part of the course where he runs in the company of one of the great local runners.

Still today on some mornings in that dangerous corner one can see him on the horns, inches from injury, racing with destiny. In the beginning, when he was a kid, he ran like that every day and always he ran at Matt's side or a step off of Matt's pace, literally following in Carney's footsteps. That was long ago, though sometimes Joe's youthful looks make one forget how much time has passed since then.

For many years Joe has shared his Pamplona apartment with David Crockett and his wife Stacey. Davey Crockett is this fellow's real name and he is a long-time veteran of Fiesta who knows Pamplona well. Davey normally attends other ferias in Spain and France. When not following the bulls, Crockett is on the Pacific in his sailboat or in the mountains on horses with pack animals. He is easily one of the most respected Americans in Fiesta

Stacey and David Crockett.

today. Over more than 30 years this really quiet, handsome man from Mammoth Lakes, California, has gained a reputation as a bullrunner and a person of consistent character. Whereas many Americans exaggerate their accomplishments in the encierro, Crockett does not even speak of his. If there is any friendship an American in Fiesta values above all others it is Crockett's. In his presence one cannot speak ill of anyone. Crockett is like a big brother in this crowd, one who can scold with a stern look. His very presence changes the character of any gathering, improving the ambiance considerably. And if one is lucky, Stacey is at his side, bringing beauty, grace, joy and laughter with her. The two of them are sometimes like an oasis of sanity in the middle of a desert of madness.

W HAT almost all Americans in Fiesta have in common is a patron or sponsor. Hardly anyone has completely figured out Fiesta on their own. Some were brought into Fiesta by their parents and a large number of American regulars were stationed in Europe in the military when they stumbled into Pamplona. Most have had one or more veterans show them the way; people encountered in chance meetings in pensions, on the plaza, in an airport or crowded café.

Without the generosity of such a person, a true patron, on a first visit, it is probable that few would ever return. This tradition of generosity can be traced back to Matt Carney.

One American who had no patron when he first arrived in Spain, no help of any kind, one who did it his way on his own was Matador John Fulton, a man whose achievements are starkly different from those of Hemingway, Carney and Distler. Matador de Toros Fulton lived his adult life in Sevilla, Spain as a bullfighter, illustrator, painter, sculptor and designer of the suits worn by matadors. His art is in the collections of the Vatican, the Michener and Hemingway estates, and it is installed in permanent exhibitions in museums in Spain, Mexico and the United States.

Fulton fought in bullrings on two continents in a career spanning 41 years. He had the occasion to share cartels with some of the leading matadors of the day, including El Cordobes and Antonio Ordóñez. Fulton's association with and participation in Fiesta primarily revolved around his appearances in Pamplona as a bullfighter, fighting bulls in festivales, though he also ran the bulls and acted as a Fiesta guide for his longtime friend, James Michener, during the author's research for *Iberia*.

COLLECTION OF MATADOR JOHN FULTON

Author James A. Michener with Matador John Fulton on Plaza del Castillo in 1966 while Fulton was Michener's guide during research for Iberia. *Fulton loved the photo, which shows the millionaire writer wearing a cheap Timex wristwatch while the starving artist and out-of-work torero sports an expensive, stylish Swiss timepiece.*

As a matador he never received accolades, however, as a man few denied him the dignity and honor he earned and deserved. He had many heroes, historic figures from all walks of life, and he admired a narrow range of Mexican and Spanish matadors. He identified closely with Harper Lee, an American

OPPOSITE PAGE: *Matador John Fulton in his prime, wearing a suit of lights of his own design.*

who was a matador well before Fulton's time. Visiting Harper Lee's widow, John received gifts that included Lee's coleta or pigtail, the caste mark of a killer of bulls. Like Lee before him, he was alone in a profession that can be lonely even when one has an entourage. His life in the taurine world was truly a valiant struggle against unimaginable odds.

A great irony in John's life is that he rarely received the support one might expect him to receive from English speaking aficionados. There were those in that crowd who disparaged him as a bullfighter when he was not around, talking behind his back. These same people would never have found the courage in a thousand years to make one single cape pass with a four year old toro bravo. He had devoted his entire life to doing something they only watched. Some of these same people, and John knew who they were, loved to take him to dinner and be entertained by his stories. Whenever this hypocrisy was discussed in his presence, John grinned and shrugged. He never had ill will toward anyone and he never talked about people. He was secure in his accomplishments and needed no validation from anyone.

Fulton is the only American ever elevated to the rank of matador de toros in Spain through the formal ceremony known as the *alternativa*. His induction was held in the Real Maestranza bullring in Sevilla, and he received confirmation of that ceremony in the most important bullring in the world, in Madrid. When he died suddenly in February 1998 of a heart attack, John was writing a memoir. The story was finished in a way in a lovely book, *Our Friend John Fulton "Quixote"*, written by his longtime friend and fellow matador, Curro Camacho, whose collaborator and translator was the lady of Fulton's life, Judy Cotter, the one who had Fulton's parade cape draped over the railing of her front row seat during his last bullfight.

John believed in impossible dreams, dreams he lived. His very life was art. His dream was born in the 1940s in a movie theater in a working class neighborhood of Philadelphia while watching Tyrone Power in *Blood and Sand* on a Saturday night. Fulton was just a kid as he sat in the dim, flickering light of that cinema house. His mother sent him to the movies in her place on dish night. Each week patrons were given a new dish, and his mom wanted to have the whole set. He returned home late, having watched the movie twice. His mother got her dish and John got his dream that night, and an impossible dream it was. From that day, this fair-haired handsome American set out on a quest to convince the Spanish taurine world that he was a torero. After a lengthy and monumental struggle, John became a torero.

He made his living through his art gallery in the center of Sevilla. His best-known works are blood paintings made in the tradition of the ancient cave paintings of Altamira that depict aurochs, ancestors of today's fighting bull. For these works Fulton used

Matadors Juan Belmonte and John Fulton in profile. Belmonte revolutionized the art of toreo during his era, establishing himself as a grand figura of all epochs. Tha great Spanish matador liked Fulton, was a good friend and strong supporter of the young gringo torero.

the blood of bulls he killed in the ring. He was equally well known for the elaborate, original images he created for *cartels* or posters used to announce bullfights in Spain, France and Mexico. The works of art that secured his permanent place in the Ronda Bullfighting Museum are his designs for the suits worn by men who fight bulls.

The subjects and scope of Fulton's art extended far beyond the bullring to drawings, illustrations, paintings, etchings, portraits, pieces with mythological themes, landscapes and works of fantasy. He was an inventor and creator of large sculptures, and he also worked as a metalsmith making delicate jewelry. His illustrated book *Bullfighting*, which he always described as a primer, is probably the best basic book ever written in the English language on the corrida.

Fulton's tour as a torero ended in the spring of 1994, his

farewell season as a matador. That spring, at 61, an age when most men are pensioned, he fought three bullfights in less than three weeks. In the last week of his career he faced, fought and killed four bulls in four days. In each bullfight he was awarded at least one ear and the plaza band played *Las Golondrinas* for him, a traditional, stirring farewell song.

A classic John Fulton painting of a toro bravo. This one is painted in bull's blood, a technique Fulton developed after visiting the caves with James Michener and studying the medium used to make the paintings on stone that have lasted centuries.

In the Yucatan, John made a triumphant tour of the ring in a driving rain with gale force winds whipping off the sea. An old newspaper critic and friend of John's who had known him since he first arrived in Mexico 40 years earlier was moved to tears. He stepped out from under the dry cover where he had been standing. They embraced and laughed like two men sharing a private joke.

Fulton's *despedida*, or formal retirement corrida, was scheduled for Easter in San Miguel de Allende where he had studied art and learned to fight bulls under the elegant torero Pepe Ortiz and the Mexican figura Luis Procuna. On Holy Saturday in San Miguel, John would once more step onto the sand of the same plaza where he first wore a traje de luces and cut an ear in the summer of 1953. Friends from all over the world assembled in this picturesque setting, a colonial town hanging on a high hill north of Mexico City.

Wearing the traditional attire a matador dons in the campo or countryside, Matador John Fulton drinks wine from a bota after testing two-year-old cows at Tenexac, a bull ranch in the mountains of central Mexico.

The American Pamplona crowd was well represented for Fulton's farewell performance. Barnaby Conrad, an author with impeccable taurine credentials, flew in from California with a group of friends and joined American film director Tony Brand and others on the eve of the bullfight. Joe Distler, Allen Josephs, Tom Turley and Robin Kelley O'Connor were seated directly behind the matador. The ring was sold out, standing room only. People without tickets stood on nearby rooftops to see the corrida.

JANIS HEYMANN

Matador John Fulton on a Mexican ganaderia with Manolo Montes, a novice Fulton called the "taxi torero" because he drove a Mexico City cab during the week. On weekends Montes would sneak the taxi out to bull ranches for tientas where Fulton trained him as he worked with wild vacas, young cows.

Sharing the card with Fulton in his last appearance in San Miguel de Allende was Mariano Ramos, an accomplished matador who had killed more than two thousand bulls.

The stage was nearly set. Phone calls, faxes and telegrams came in from friends around the world. Noel Chandler called from Singapore. In Austin, James Michener assembled a prayer group and waited by the phone for a report from his friend, while John's first art teacher Isa Barnett waited anxiously in Santa Fe.

The mood among Fulton's friends in San Miguel was a mixture of celebration and apprehension. Some of them killed time before the bullfight by milling about the art institute where a retrospective exhibition of Fulton's art was on display. Some sat in cool cafés all afternoon. Most of John's friends knew that matadors usually retire in their forties, many do so in their thirties and some even earlier. Some friends knew that John had trouble with his feet and legs. They knew he could easily be caught by a bull, be seriously injured, or worse.

Time passed slowly in the hours before Fulton's final corrida. John dressed in a home across the street from the bullring. As he stepped into a brilliant traje de luces tailored in Spain specifically for this day, the bullring band began to play in the street beneath his window. A few close friends were with him when he walked down the steps to the foyer. There he paused and took a deep breath. There was applause as the door opened and he exited the house. With long strides, he walked toward the main entrance to the plaza. As he approached the bullring, the band began *Las Golondrinas* and the crowd stepped back, making way for him. At the gate he paused to accept hugs, kisses and good wishes from friends who spanned his whole life. Then he took the long walk to the callejón and donned the parade cape now in the Ronda museum.

The stage was set. Fulton would appear in a suit of lights for the last time on Easter Saturday in the same ring where he wore a traje de luces the first time. The last bull he would kill in 1994 would be from the same ranch as the first bull he fought in 1953, Santacilia.

Then the corrida unfolded. Those who saw it have talked about the bullfight for years. Both Allen Josephs and Joe Distler have written eloquent accounts of the afternoon in San Miguel. It had everything: danger, bravery and art. Everyone who knew John knew this was one of his dreams, the dream of a little boy in Philadelphia so long ago, a dream of returning to where it all began and ending his career in triumph. And for a few minutes with his last bull, in the faena, John looked like that fair-haired teenage kid from Philadelphia.

The matador triumphed in San Miguel. The president of the plaza awarded two ears. John stood alone in the center of the arena with his son. Federico reached up and cut John's *coleta*, the pigtail which is the caste mark of the matador. In this moment, the final moment of his career, there was a blending of time and tradition. Everything was in the present. In Fulton's features one could clearly see traces of the little boy who once fought imaginary bulls with a barber's cloth. He was carried out of the plaza on shoulders, over the sand he first set foot on 41 years before.

Of Fulton's final fight, famed author of books on bullfighting, Barnaby Conrad was to write: *The Despedida of John Fulton*

I saw Cañitas and Félix Guzmán in a great *mano a mano* in Mexico, 1941.

I saw Chicuelo fight one of his last fights in Sevilla in 1943.

I saw Belmonte and El Gallo in a historic festival in Sevilla, 1944.

I saw the great Manolete, Arruza and Pepe Luís Vásquez' *corrida* in Sevilla in the Sevilla Feria, 1945.

I saw Luís Procuna in his heart-stopping performance in Lima, 1946.

I saw Antonio Ordóñez with the enshrined bull Cascabel, Mexico City, 1956.

But none of these fantastic afternoons was more emotional than seeing John Fulton thumb his nose at both age and adversity and triumph in San Miguel de Allende in 1994.

ONE of the most important figures in the American taurine experience was a school teacher from Milledgeville, Georgia. In the sixties Michener recognized her in *Iberia* as one of the foremost living authorities on bulls and bullfighting. Spanish author Jose Antonio de Moral dedicated a bullfighting book to her in part, *Como ver una corrida de toros*, and her birthdays were noted in Spanish bullfight periodicals.

Alice Hall carved out a unique niche in a foreign world and positioned herself there without yielding to the obvious conventions of her own culture. At a time when women in her homeland did not travel across their home state alone, Alice was crisscrossing a foreign country following bullfight fiestas.

She traveled the bullfight season for nearly 50 years until her death at 90. As she approached her tenth decade her only concession to age was to shorten her annual stay in Spain to five months.

No foreign woman before her ever attained a more prominent place in the taurine world. She knew toreo, everything about it and everyone in it, and everyone knew that. She was as opinionated about toreo as she was about all things in her life. She did not suffer fools.

Once toward the end of her life I spent a week with her in Burgos during the Feria of San Pedro. The San Pedro fiesta often bumps up against Pamplona's Sanfermines on the calendar. We were the only two of our crowd in that beautiful city. It was a week of rain and cold weather which canceled most of the corridas, and when bullfights were held they were unremarkable and muddy. That week all there was for me was the magnificent Burgos cathedral and Miss Hall, two very different monuments. Having Alice's company was more than enough. We both stayed in Hotel España and developed a daily routine.

Alice had a commanding presence and it seemed that her frail legs were the only things in life that did not obey her commands. She used a cane, and in the afternoons we had trouble boarding the bus to the bullfight. I would have to pick her up like a child to get her onto the bus to the corrida and afterwards I had to offload her less delicately. The bus did not stop for very long and as it jammed its brakes I would almost throw or pitch Alice to the sidewalk. She would laugh, recover her dignity and march on undaunted, head held high.

In the evenings we almost always had dinner together at a small café peopled by players in the world of bullfighting and filled with that unique ambience. During dinner Alice very patiently fielded my questions about matadors Ordóñez, Dominguín, Antoinette, Curro Romero, Paco Camino and the evolution of different breeds of bulls. She would answer my questions and then launch into a long discourse about her favorite matadors, especially Espla, who had painted her portrait that spring, a painting she traveled with all summer and displayed in her hotel room. She loved matador Ruiz Miguel and was looking forward to his appearance in Pamplona with Miura bulls. Alice never tired of talking about toreo, though she bored of speaking about herself.

As the week went on in an unraveling string of disappointments, Alice began to look longingly at the San Fermín poster which dominated the wall of the small bar where we spent much of our time. The bar's patrons, like the men in the café where we had meals, were people who loved the bullfight. Critics, men who write about la fiesta brava, sat at a corner table and played cards, smoking cigars and gambling for drinks as the rain continued. Matadors and their entourages came through the bar some nights.

On nights when bullfighters and their cuadrillas came into the bar they would walk by our table single file, approaching Alice like altar boys before a bishop. Their conversation was quiet. There seemed to be more reverence and respect for her than affection. Though they knew her, few of them were her close friends.

Her friendships with toreros were based more on their personal qualities than their performance in the ring. Once Alice extended friendship to a matador she remained loyal to him, yet always honest in her appraisal of his performance. She could be very critical and at her age some-times the criticism she handed out could come off as cranki-ness. It seemed that some of the toreros felt they had escaped when they walked away. There were times when Alice, like a lot of elderly people, did not allow room for discussion or debate of ideas that did not coincide with her opinions.

On these nights

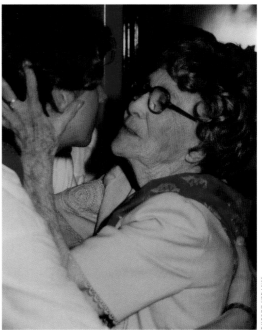

Alice Hall embraces young Todd Mouton in one of her last fiestas. Her great beauty, charisma, and passion for life are evident in this photograph.

when the toreros were in the café a young boy would stand in the center of the street in the rain. We could all see him through the large plate glass window. He would make passes with an old, dirty cape and a muleta given him by a torero after it was worn out. Alice knew him, this kid, a boy of maybe 14. He had been following bullfight fiestas for two seasons, showing off his stuff in the street, hoping a matador or a manager would be impressed. Alice said sometimes the boy slept on the floors of hotel rooms where members of matadors' cuadrillas stayed. She said some picadors and banderilleros were kind and remembered their own youthful aspirations. They would allow him a place to sleep and shower and provide pesetas for meals. Mostly the boy slept in the street.

The image of this boy fashioning a fantasy faena in a driving rain haunted me all that week and it has never left me. I've seen him several times since then, always in the sun. Each time he was carrying a matador around the ring on his shoulders. This is as close as he has come to his dream of glory.

Alice enjoyed the young aspirants as much as she enjoyed the skeptical old critics. She shared the dreams of the young ones and the cynicism of the old ones. She hoped each day that the corrida would be wonderful and at the same time often doubted it would be anything like the bullfights she had seen in days gone by.

One evening as the rain poured in sheets off the awning of the small bar Alice picked up her cane and pointed to the cartel poster advertising San Fermín. Then, with the tip of her cane, she very slowly tapped the printed letters spelling out P A M P L O N A.

As Alice's cane struck the poster on the wall she said in her very rich, soft southern accent, "Oh get me out of Burgos, Ray Mouton. Bring me to my Pamplona. Bring me to San Fermín where the bulls have horns."

Miss Hall's tiny figure cut a wide path through Pamplona and the rest of the taurine world. Alice loved San Fermín, even the racket and tacky behavior she complained about so often. One Fiesta evening at dinner in the lovely Europa restaurant I saw Alice hurry to a set of French doors and struggle with stubborn and difficult door latches. She threw the doors open so she could get to the balcony outside. Below, two peña bands had run head on in a narrow street. Standing their ground and keeping time, each band played its own tune as loudly as possible. Alice stood there framed by the doorway to the balcony pounding her cane in time with one hand, her free hand waving above her head, dancing in the only way she could. She was 83 then.

At my parents' home in Louisiana I once heard Alice ask for a Bourbon and branch water. Her accent as well as her phrasing were from a place and time I never knew except through the works of William Faulkner and Tennessee Williams. She seemed rooted in another time and place.

One evening in Burgos over coffee after dinner, as she allowed herself her only cigarette of the day, a strong one made of black tobacco, I asked her how one can arrange one's life as she had arranged hers. How does one live this way, do these things in these places in this style?

Alice's response to my question about her life was a long one. I recall her saying that she did not feel her life was so remarkable. She said, "Some women raise families, some raise flowers, some sew dresses, some have professions and some cheat at cards. I go to the bulls."

Alice laughed and agreed with me when I suggested that going to the bulls was more like cheating at cards than planting flowers. But it was that simple to her. I do not think anything in life was ever very complicated for Alice. She said that people just have to decide in life, and that many never decide. That you have to decide what you want to do, how you want to live. When you know what you want something will surround you and your life and this will attract things you need and repel things you don't need.

She felt most people go through life never knowing what they want and live and die feeling unfulfilled, never knowing why they feel so unfulfilled, what it was they wanted and missed. Miss Hall knew what she wanted in life and she got it all.

Her death, like her life, had great dignity. A long-time afficionado and dear friend of Alice's who has attended major bullfight ferias for years and not missed Pamplona in ages, Chris Humphreys, was with her not long before she died. Humphreys' report was that she was content. Alice was diagnosed with a problem that had no cure. She rested comfortably in Georgia for a short time. She did not linger. With dignity, grace, beauty, confidence and courage, she faced death like the toros and toreros she so loved. She fielded calls and correspondence from around the world, expressions of love, and then passed on.

Miss Hall died quietly in a winter between bull seasons. It was the end of an era. She was the last of her generation. When summer came there was yet another new generation of Americans arriving at the train depot and bus station in Pamplona, some of whom would carry on in the tradition of Alice Hall though they had never heard of her.

Chris Humphreys wearing the pañuelo given to him in 1972 by a lovely young Basque woman from Vitoria. His old, faded scarf was immortalized in 1993 when it was featured on the official Fiesta poster.

O F ALL THE PLACES Ernest Hemingway loved best that have been modernized and transformed into a mecca for tourists, Pamplona remains the most unchanged. Cuba is not open yet, but Idaho is a ski resort, Key West is an upscale playground, Paris leads the world in tourism, and a roaring lion in Africa draws ten busloads of tourists within minutes. But in Pamplona they still run the bulls up Estafeta in the morning and dance on Estafeta all night just as they did in 1923. Here there is a sense of another time, a time we all imagine was a better time. For a few days each year romantics live in that time. And when the reality does not match the romance, you

must find it within
yourself.

As things were
coming to a close on
the last day of Fiesta
2001 and this book
was finishing, my
friend Joe Riehl and I
took a long siesta
through the after-
noon in our hotel
room. Late in the day
when we met up with
my wife Melony and
her friend Lisa Goda,

*Melony and Ray Mouton share a laugh in the bullring
after a corrida.*

the wind coming off the foothills was gusting and black clouds were
racing across the sky.

That morning the women had attended mass at the Chapel of
San Fermín in the San Lorenzo church. There they heard something
about the cancellation of festivities. Our neighbor in the hotel,
Desmond Boylan with Reuters News, explained that ETA terrorists
had exploded a car bomb earlier that morning in a nearby village. At
least one person had been killed. The candlelight closing ceremony
had been canceled by the mayor and town council. Their actions
were taken out of respect for the victims and their families.

It looked like the worst kind of weather for a bullfight, weather
not bad enough to cancel the corrida and allow you to hurry out of
the rain to a nice bar or restaurant, but just bad enough to make the
sand a mess and all but guarantee a below-average bullfight. We made
a plan on the way to the bullring and secured seats at the top of the
plaza in the grada alta section under a roof so we would not get wet if
rain came. The rain threatened through the first bulls. Joe was fasci-
nated by the animals. They were Miura bulls, unlike any Joe had seen
all week in that they seemed to transmit a greater sense of danger
and violence. The animals were bravo or wild, magnificent, and in a

word which is not a word at all, they were nearly unfightable. It is often difficult for a matador to fashion an artistic faena with a Miura. It was going all right until a brave matador named Padilla was gored through the neck. It was a horrific injury. The bloody, life-threatening goring and the dark cloud hanging above the bullring put a pallor on a Fiesta that was not ending well. Then the rain began.

Traditionally on July 14 when the last bull has been dragged out of the ring and the matadors have exited the plaza, the peñas stay in their seats for an hour or more playing music that is alternately stirring and sentimental. The whole plaza stays in their seats for this informal concert. The feeling one has as the music pours forth from the penas is a combination of what one feels on New Year's Eve and the emotions felt at a funeral.

On this day, the crowd that usually stays for the music rushed out of the rain, jamming the exit portals as the last bull fell. Even some of the peña bands stopped playing and began climbing down out of the stands onto the sand to leave the arena through the main gate. We walked down to the first row of the grada, the highest section. Safe from the falling rain, we stood and watched the peñas. When the wind shifted, light rain blew into our faces. Thunder resounded somewhere in the distance, then lightning split the dark sky. It was going to storm.

I felt a tap on my shoulder and I turned to see a lovely young woman. The first thing I noticed about her, even before realizing how pretty she was, were her whites, still in pristine condition. No one on July 14, especially given the rain and grime in the streets that day, has clean clothes. "I'm Elizabeth Kraft," she said.

I looked at her, and I am sure I must have smiled. I could not believe the moment - could not believe I was encountering this young woman in this setting. I know Pamplona brings many people together. It was here that I came to know Miss Hall, John Fulton, Matt Carney, Tom Turley, David Crockett and many others. Little in Fiesta should be able to surprise you. In Pamplona, some say "there are no coincidences in Fiesta." Many believe there are no coincidences in life.

Hearing her name, seeing her face stunned me. I knew who Elizabeth was. She's from the town I was raised in. I've known her mother all my life, and I danced at the wedding of her parents. In her face I thought I saw her mother's eyes and her father's smile. Maybe it was the other way around. She had a presence, a wholesomeness about her which I knew was also inherited.

Speechless for a moment, I looked up at her and said, "I don't believe I have ever seen you. But, you know, I knew you existed." It must have sounded silly, but it was true. I remember all the excitement surrounding her arrival in the Kraft house. Elizabeth laughed and told me that when she told her parents she was coming to Pamplona they told her I would be here. She thought she would never run into me, and I'm not sure she had any idea of how long the odds of us meeting at this time and place were. Had it not been threatening rain, we would not have been sitting so near her in the bullring.

Elizabeth told me she was studying law at LSU. I too was an LSU law student when I first came to Fiesta, and I was her age back then also, so many years ago. I don't remember what else we talked about. It wasn't a long conversation. I introduced Melony and we said goodbye. In those few moments I spent with Elizabeth and her friends from the university I began to miss my own children and was reminded of Fiestas with them when they were her age and a lot younger. None of my kids were in Pamplona this Fiesta.

As Melony and I walked out of the portal onto the terrace that wraps around the ring we were more exposed to the weather. Off toward the mountains the thunder continued. I walked to the stone railing and looked down at the river. The wind was blowing and bending the trees growing in the shallows. I could barely make out an old grove of tall trees with big leaves set back from the river on higher ground. It was in these trees, on the banks of the river behind the bullring that we parked the green Volkswagen station wagon and camped out during Fiesta in 1970. Moments from that first Pamplona adventure with my army buddy Jack Cooper, my first wife Janis and our 21-month-old son Todd, flooded through my memory. For a long time I looked down at the river, trying to find the exact place where we made camp. Lost in my search, my feelings, and memories, I didn't realize the rain was beginning to beat against my face. Melony took my hand and we started down the concrete stairwell. I was unusually quiet.

She asked if I was okay. I was okay. Meeting Elizabeth had delighted me. The day began with a terrorist car bomb exploding not long after the rocket fired for the encierro, then storm clouds from the sea rolled over the foothills and blanketed the town and we were witness to a dull corrida with little art and a terrible injury to a torero, after which rain ruined the concert of the peñas, and that evening there would be no candlelight closing ceremony with music before the town hall. Seeing Elizabeth had triggered something deep within me for it was something like a closing circle where in my heart I met myself again as I once was when I was her age. The things I had allowed to cloud my mind all afternoon in the way storm clouds filled the sky, the way I had allowed the negative events of the day to impact me, were giving way to the things that now filled my heart. And Fiesta is about the heart, all of it is about the heart. It is our hearts that carry us through the days and nights of Fiesta and beyond.

As we made our way down the tiers of stairs I could really remember my first trip to Pamplona when I had been Elizabeth's age. I could remember how we all looked then, how we laughed then. That first Fiesta came for me in that time all of us have but once, that time between adolescence and adulthood, the advent of our lives, the time before anything bad has happened.

I could also remember random things from all the years of Fiesta since then: a family picnic in the Pyrenees, seeing Fulton the first time running bulls in a plaid shirt and wearing aviator sunglasses, watching Matt circle the outdoor cafés with an armload of roses and giving one to every female, watching the night crossing from the wall with Jesse, sitting the bulls with Joe, seeing Crockett run bulls without ever looking back, following Noel and a peña into the dawn and sharing a sunrise breakfast in Chandler's flat.

Outside the bullring Melony and I swung around to the

Hemingway statue to tell the old man goodbye. My son Chad tells me that we should always look at everyone and everything we see as if it is both the first and last time we will see them. I do this every year when Fiesta is ending. I look at all of Pamplona this way as Sanfermines draws to a close.

The next morning the sky was blue, the town quiet as it always is following Fiesta. Leaving Pamplona we followed the same trace we travel every year. On our way to Roncesvalles Pass through the Pyrenees we stopped at Restaurant Beti Jai in Aoiz, an unlikely locale in which to find a place that rivals any restaurant in Europe in terms of ambiance, food and service. The lovely English-speaking daughter of the owner, Izaskun Iturri, translates the menu for foreigners.

After lunch in Aoiz, we made our way to Hotel du Palais in Biarritz where we had a drink on the south terrace with Jean-Louis Leimbacher, the director of the hotel, an afficionado whose favorite torero is Enrique Ponce. Jean-Louis and I talked bulls, then he and Melony talked about the flowers in the hotel garden. Finishing his drink and promising to go to a corrida with us at week's end in Bayonne, Jean-Louis wandered toward the pool deck.

In Biarritz the sun sets in the sea, beyond the Bay of Biscay that lies in front of Hotel Du Palais, a grand palace originally constructed by Napoleon III as a summer home for his wife Eugenie. At dusk sunlight slowly gives way to the glow of lights along the beach promenade that traces the small cove around which the town is centered. The lamp in the lighthouse that sits on a high cliff illuminates a signal that can be seen as far away as Spain, and a star or planet rises in the distance, a celestial presence that always seems to hang over the horizon off the French coast at this time of year. The hard west wind that causes the surf to crash against huge rocks at high tide slackens to a gentle breeze at last light. We were alone on the hotel terrace by the sea, watching this dramatic scene change in this enchanted place. It was quiet.

Warm feelings welled within me as I allowed myself to think of absent friends, people whose funerals were as different as their lives. Alice Hall's last rites were in the tradition of the deep South,

Matt Carney was laid to rest on a high point on the Irish coast, and John Fulton's coffin was carried into the bullring in Sevilla. Whenever I think of Alice I can see Miss Hall shaking her finger in my face, scolding me like the school teacher she was, dressing me down for forgetting to mail something to her or do something else I promised. One of my fondest memories of John is the image I have of him dressing for his final corrida, laughing easily as he tucked a note from my teenage daughter in his waistband, a hand-scribbled line that read "Rock 'n' roll dreams really do come true." And I will always remember Matt laughing and waltzing, dancing every dance in a Cajun dance hall, on a night when only he knew his death was imminent.

Funerals and fiestas. Someone once said that is all life is, just funerals and fiestas. That night on the hotel terrace in Biarritz I had lived long enough to have experienced a lot of fiestas and too many funerals. The people I thought about then - Alice, Matt and John - understood better than anyone I have known, the importance of fiestas, the necessity of living full out for a few days, celebrating life, embracing life all the tighter. Outside of fiesta, this trio lived their lives in an uncompromising way. They were not bound by barriers of convention or custom, and they were free of the fears that rule the lives of so many.

All three were dreamers with very different dreams, and they pursued their dreams. A female school teacher from a small, conservative Georgia town became one of the most knowledgeable people in the world about a foreign art form that is dominated by men. A little boy from Philadelphia grew up to wear a suit of lights and fight bulls in Sevilla and Madrid. An ex-GI lived out his life as an expatriate, studying and writing philosophy and literature, and he became legendary for being the first foreigner to consistently do a dangerous thing exceedingly well in an elegant way that was uniquely his own.

Their dreams were truly impossible dreams, pursued in the face of seemingly insurmountable odds. At the end of their lives they had a sense of satisfaction and contentment that eludes many people as they face death. It is true that Matt did not achieve the

kind of success as a writer he dreamed of, and John's ten-
torero fell far short of his ambitious vision, and maybe the
things Alice wanted in life that did not come her way. The
peace they all experienced toward the end of their lives w:
result of them having fully achieved their dreams, but
rather a result of them having pursued those dreams.

Melony walked down to the beach while I was lost in
thought. She waved to me and I stood to join her. As I
reached for my small notebook on the table, I saw where I
had scribbled the name Elizabeth Kraft with a note
reminding me to call her parents. I closed the notebook
and tucked it in the pocket of my jacket. As I looked to
the beach, the sun was fast disappearing in distant swells.
I thought about this lovely young lady from the south,
Elizabeth, and I thought of Alice Hall, another southern
lady from a different time. And I thought of all the young
people of Elizabeth's generation I had seen wandering
across the cobblestones all week in Pamplona, the true
stars of the American experience in Fiesta.

After having allowed myself to spend time thinking
of people whose lives were now in the past, I focused for a
moment on those whose whole lives lay before them. I
hoped each of them would find their own dream and pur-
sue the dream throughout their lives, for if there is any
true legacy handed down through the continuum of the
American experience it is a romantic legacy that very
much involves loyalty to one's dream. When I thought of
the young ones and all those who had gone before them, I
also thought of Hemingway and of Ecclesiastes and how
"One generation passeth away, and another generation
cometh."

We were alone on our end of the beach. It was now
dark. Behind us, a group of young surfers sat in a circle on
the sand. A light breeze carried their laughter out to sea.
We walked in the direction of the lighthouse, talking

about our plans for the next day. We would not talk about Fiesta again for it was now over. For us, Fiesta finally finishes when we have crossed the mountains to another country.

Biarritz, France at last light.

1948 Cartel

GLOSSARY

Abono: A season ticket. In Pamplona an abono allows entry to a reserved seat for each bullfight during Fiesta. Over half the seats in the bullring are reserved as abonos, which are difficult to obtain as most abonos have been held for years. Applicants often have to wait several years on a list. Anyone not claiming his or her abono before July 6 automatically loses it and his or her place is taken by the next person on the waiting list.

Adornos: Unnecessary flourishes added to capework or muleta passes by a matador, and flamboyant gestures (such as patting the bull's nose, or kneeling and resting an elbow on the animal's head) on the part of the matador which form part of a style of bullfighting called tremendista. These flourishes and gestures, generally frowned upon by critics and purists, are sometimes incorporated into the work of well-respected matadors, and when used sparingly and respectfully are acceptable.

Aficionado: A knowledgeable fan or member of the cognoscenti of what the Spanish call la fiesta brava, or the bullfight. More than simply passion for or love of the corrida, this term first implies in-depth knowledge. Without this knowledge one might be attracted to the pageantry alone, as some are drawn to opera without understanding the language of the drama or its story line. Humorously and accurately, Matador John Fulton once described an aficionado as one who completely understands bullfighting and nevertheless likes it. The term is also used to describe or denote an amateur bullfighter.

Aqua: Water.

Aqua del grifo: Tap water as opposed to mineral water. Many travelers fear tap water in foreign countries, but tap water in Pamplona is among the best one can find: cool, rich in minerals and marked by a distinctive and pleasing taste.

Alegría: Sense of joy. A difficult word to define for the feeling it describes is one which wells deep within a person and is easily sensed by those around them. It is far more than happiness and is almost a centered, spiritual soundness and completeness, a unity of one with life and his or her surroundings.

Alguaciles: Horsemen who lead the paseo or parade at the start of the bullfight and act as functionaries for the president of the bullring, handing over the keys for the opening of the toril, or gate, from which the bulls are released and making the award of trophies to the matador in the form of the bull's ears, tail and sometimes hooves.

Alternativa: The ceremony graduating a novice torero or novillero to the status of matador de toros in a bullfight which is the first time the novillero alternates with full matadors on a cartel in a formal corrida. It is a formal ceremony of the handing over of the sword. Very few who aspire to become matadors ever reach this level and then only with a combination of great talent, serious financial backing, good connections in the taurine world, and luck. Often the ceremony is in the bullring of the city or region where the novillero was born, and occasionally the young man's padrino or sponsor will be a senior matador who has been his hero since childhood. The date of the event will determine the younger bullfighter's rank in terms of seniority for the remainder of his career as a torero.

Apartado: After the sorteo, around midday, the bulls are moved from a communal corral to individual pens under the plaza de toros in this public event that requires a ticket and is often attended by aficionados who want a close look at the bulls to know more about the protagonists of the afternoon's corrida.

Auroch: An ancient animal depicted in cave paintings; the historical ancestor of the toro bravo or fighting bull of today. A distinct physical resemblance can be seen and undoubtedly the spirit of the beast and fighting bull are similar.

Ayuntamiento: Though the term can mean town council, in this volume it is a reference to Pamplona's town hall. The word is of Arabic derivation and really refers to the institution rather than the building which is formally known as Casa Consistorial. Fiesta begins and ends with ceremonies in front of the town hall, when rockets are lighted by the mayor or an honoree.

Banderillas: Colorfully wrapped wooden sticks about an arm's length long with sharp spear-like barbs on the end that are placed in the area of a bull's morrillo during the second act of the corrida in a deadly ballet harkening back to ancient rites in Crete. As a result of serious injuries from banderillas hitting matadors in their eyes and necks, regulation banderillas were changed in the nineties to a type that can flex at a place just above the barbed point. Now, after a few shakes of the bull's head or a couple of passes by the matador, the sticks lay flat against the bull's hide for the remainder of the corrida.

Banderillero: A title held by three members of a matador's cuadrilla, men who may or may not place banderillas during the corrida, since sometimes the matador will do this himself. During the second act of the bullfight, a total of three sets of two banderillas will usually be placed.

Barrio: Neighborhood; not necessarily a poor area, though that can be the connotation of the word in some American cities. In pre-medieval times the historic district of Pamplona, where Fiesta is centered, was divided into small districts called burgos, which were enclosed by their own walls. They were often in violent conflict with each other. The modern barrios of San Jorge, San Juan, Iturrama, La Txantrea and La Rotxapea are situated just outside the old town and were built over the last 80 years as the population of Pamplona increased eight-fold.

Basque: A people and a language, as well as a people who define themselves by their language as in "She is a speaker of Basque" which means that "She is Basque." The language originally spoken by most of the inhabitants of the Spanish provinces of Guipuzcoa, Alava, Vizcaya and Navarra as well as the French provinces of Labourd, Basse Navarre and Soultine. Medieval records suggest that Basque may have also been spoken in some parts of the provinces of Burgos, Rioja and Huesca in ancient times as well.

Basque is a non-Indo European language and is not related to any other Western European language. Its origins are unknown. The first books in Basque, including a translation of the New Testament and a book of religious poetry entitled Gero, were published in France in the mid-seventeenth century. The Basque language suffered a gradual decline in the modern era but has recently enjoyed a renaissance on the Spanish side of the border both as a literary and spoken language. It is widely spoken in the mountainous northwest area of Navarra.

Many Pamplona residents would consider themselves Basque, but most would not. Many famous Spaniards were Basques including the founder of the Jesuits, Ignacio Loyola, the famous revolutionary "La Pasionara" and the novelist Pío Baroja. Today there are approximately 500,000 Basque speakers in Spain, France, the United States and South America.

Bota: A cured wineskin featuring a narrow nozzle at one end from which wine is squirted. Without a properly made bota and the knowledge and time needed to cure it, the user will experience a taste similar to that which might be found if one were to drink from an old baseball glove. Botas usually make better souvenirs than drinking equipment.

Brindis: The matador's dedication, in which the bull's imminent death is dedicated to a close friend, relative or some dignitary in the crowd. The brindis may also be made to the crowd in general. A matador will make no brindis or dedication except in circumstances where he feels what he has observed and experienced with the bull during the cape work, pic-ing, and placing of the banderillas indicates the potential of a triumph with the bull is probable. The brindis is made hat in hand, as the matador extends his montera, or hat, in front of him toward those who receive the dedication. Sometimes a brief verbal dedication is delivered. When the matador chooses not to dedicate the faena, he will simply hand his montera over the barrera or fence to his manager or a member of his cuadrilla and approach the bull directly in a businesslike manner.

Burladero: A portion of the wooden barrera, or barrier, circling the sand of the bullring that stands out alone in the sand a short distance to protect an opening in the wall. A torero can slip behind a burladero to make a dignified exit from the sand during a corrida. Often more hurried, less dignified exits are made by toreros when they vault the barrera with a bull inches behind them. Burladeros also provide quick access to the ring for members of the cuadrilla in critical times when they must rush onto the sand to save a downed matador. In those instances they almost fly onto the sand with large capes waving in an effort to distract the bull's attention.

Cabestros: Steers. In all bullrings these animals are trained, kept and maintained by the plaza de toros to be used to herd a bull out of the ring if it is injured, cowardly, rejected for any other reason or spared for exceptional bravery by the president of the plaza. From their earliest days, bulls follow steers and oxen and the sound of the clanging bells tied to their necks as they are moved from place to place on ranches or ganaderias, so they are in the habit of following steers peacefully. In Pamplona cabestros serve an important purpose every morning during the encierro. There are more steers than bulls in the street and they help keep the herd together. The steers run year after year, however, so after a day or two they remember the course and take the turns on the inside while the bulls always veer wide. Still, without the cabestros an encierro would not even be imaginable.

Café solo: Very strong black coffee like an Italian espresso. Like most Mediterranean people, Spaniards like their coffee strong enough to stand on its own without a cup.

Caldo: A broth or light soup made from ham bones. Sometimes mixed with a shot of dry sherry, caldo is popular with bullrunners and people who have stayed up all night in the streets. It usually first appears in Pamplona on July 8 or 9, and it is rarely served before 3 a.m.

Calle: Street. Some southern Navarran towns such as Olite still use the ancient word Rúa.

Callejón: The narrow tunnel entrance to the bullring. This last stretch of the encierro is slightly downhill and the runners sprint through deep shadows into the darker tunnel, emerging into the light when they enter the ring. Small ground-level cutouts were built into the base of the walls of the callejón to give runners some form of escape following the death of a runner near this point in 1977.

Capote: A large cape weighing seven to nine pounds that is magenta on one side and yellowish-gold on the other. The matador will use a capote in the first two acts of a corrida as will members of his cuadrilla, and some reputations have been built on the intricate, artistic cape work. The brilliant, superstitious gypsy matador, Rafael de Paula, was, like many in the taurine world, spooked by the color yellow. The inside of Rafael's capote was sky blue.

Cartel: The day's billing for the bullfight and a poster announcing that lineup, which usually matches three matadors with six bulls from the same ranch. These posters are fairly uniform today, but they were once great art, and in Pamplona this is reflected by the fact that there are always two official posters - one for the "Fiesta de San Fermín" and a second for the "Feria Del Toro" - emphasizing two very different aspects of the celebration. The

1901 Cartel

bullfight poster announces the bull breeds and/or the bullfights scheduled during Fiesta. Old Pamplona posters are available and some have become collector's items.

Casta: Physique, disposition and behavior of a bull reflective of the heritage of his bloodline. This is probably the single most important aspect of a corrida, and often it is a very subtle thing. Changes in the animals occur over years of breeding on some ranches, and these subtleties are ascertained and made note of by aficionados. A bull with good casta will exhibit the best qualities of its breed.

Chupinazo: The official start of the Sanfermines at noon July 6 when a rocket is fired from the balcony of the town hall, usually by the mayor or a senior member of the town council. The explosion is followed by calamitous singing and dancing by the thousands of young people jammed into the small square below. Similar and slightly less wild celebrations are held in the Plaza del Castillo. Like many Pamplona "traditions," this ceremony is a relatively recent innovation. The first chupinazo was held in 1941, though informal opening celebrations involving fireworks were held at midday on July 6 during the early part of the twentieth century. Many other smaller towns and cities across Navarra and Rioja have copied the tradition to signify the start of their own smaller fiestas.

Cojones: Testicles, used colloquially as in English ("Tiene cojones" - "He's got balls"). Bull testicles are sliced thinly and served as a snack at the apartado, and in some bars and restaurants.

Concurso: A competition. This term can refer to the poster contest, a photography competition or a song festival, but here it refers to a contest of bulls in an event called a festivale rather than a corrida, where six different ranches supply one bull each and an award is made to the ranch that brought the best bull of the afternoon.

Corrida de toros: Its literal meaning, a running of bulls, fell into disuse long ago, and today in common usage this term means a full bullfight with six four-year-old bulls, as opposed to a novillada with younger bulls or any other taurine event. While Pamplona may sponsor a novillada and a spectacle involving mounted bullfighters on the days leading up to the saint's day, from July 7-14 there will be a corrida de toros each afternoon.

Cuadrilla: A bullfighter's team of assistants comprised of banderilleros, picadors, his mozo de espadas and manager. The members of a cuadrilla are employed full time with matadors who fight often enough to keep such teams throughout the entire season. Aficionados follow these men and their careers.

La Curva: The 90-degree right-hand turn in the bullrun where Calle Mercaderes meets Estafeta. A serious point on the route. The extreme danger there is obvious and only the most talented runners can negotiate the terrain with the bulls. Toros often fall and become separated from the herd at this point, and then the mayhem escalates to even graver danger.

Día del Niño: A day during the Sanfermines which features special activities for children including concerts, religious services, competitions and puppet shows. Many of these events occur between 6:30 p.m. and 8:30 p.m. when the bullfight is being staged. Other children's activities take place throughout the Fiesta, including the Toro de Fuego, or fire bull, which races out of Santo Domingo past town hall every night, and the huge fireworks display that follows. Spanish children take a mid-afternoon nap and stay up late.

Dianas: A reveille; songs that are part of the traditional early morning musical wake up call played every day during Fiesta by La Pamplonesa. The town band begins promptly at 6:45 a.m. in front of the town hall and marches in a dignified manner around the streets of the old town signaling the start of a new day. They are accompanied for approximately 45 minutes by hundreds of dancers, some of whom have been in the streets all night. The exact route changes daily but it always starts at the same time and place. After July 7 there are usually peña bands in the early morning streets as well, playing dianas.

Divisa: Small ribbons displaying the colors of a bull's ranch attached to the morrillo region of the toro by a small metal barb. The divisa is attached just before the bull enters the ring by a man with a long pole on a catwalk above the chute through which the bull emerges from his dark pen into the bright sunlight of the bullring.

Dobladores: Men who play a critical role in the encierro each morning by using capes to guide the bulls across the bullring into the corrals. At least one doblador is a former matador and all of them have a great deal of experience with bulls. Though these men are dressed in jeans and sweaters and have only a large cape or capote to work with, they are charged with "catching" the bulls, grabbing their attention with the capes as they enter the bullring which is a sea of confusion with people running about. With great finesse and concentration, the dobladores lure the bulls to the opening leading to the corrals behind the ring. They have saved many a runner from serious injury by anticipating a bull's actions and intervening instantly to distract the animal from his target. They earn the applause they receive every day.

Empresario: A promoter of bullfights. These individuals are not necessarily known for their startling honesty as they work in a profession littered with broken promises and bribes. In Pamplona the organizers of the bullfights are respectable and everything about their corridas is straightforward and above board. The people responsible for the bullfights in Fiesta even

1902 Cartel

demonstrate generosity by bringing young bullfighters from Navarra into the plaza de toros to make their alternativa in this most important feria in their region. Though some never become successful they are given one or more shots before the home crowd.

Encierrillo: The night crossing of the bulls bound for the morning's encierro. When they arrive in Pamplona, the groups of bulls are kept in large corrals across the river from Santo Domingo. The night before they are due to run, the streets along their path are lined with wooden barricades and they move with cabestros through the streets, across the river and up the hill to a corral at the bottom of Santo Domingo. A limited number of spectators are allowed on the wall near the corral on Santo Domingo but only with a difficult-to-obtain security pass from the town council. The time differs a bit year to year, sometimes night to night, but is always signaled by the blowing of a ram's horn. The encierrillo is always observed in total silence and the only men in the streets are pastores, ranch hands or herders who work with bulls for a living. Anyone making noise, using a flash camera or otherwise distracting the bulls at this point would be subject to a fine and possibly a custodial sentence.

Encierro: The Spanish name for the running of the bulls, which translates literally as the "enclosing" of the bulls. In its present regulated form Pamplona's encierro dates from 1867, but records suggest some form of bullrun has taken place in Pamplona since the sixteenth century.

Daily encierros now take place in Pamplona from July 7-14. The running begins at 8 a.m., and it usually takes between two minutes and three-and-a-half minutes for the six bulls and accompanying steers to cover the half-mile course. Though it is not the only place where encierros occur - they are held in other places in Navarra, other provinces of Spain and other Hispanic countries - Pamplona's encierro is easily the most well known.

Enfermería: Literally, a hospital or emergency treatment facility in a bullring, normally located directly across from the chapel. Basic first aid and emergency care for injured matadors and bullrunners is performed free of charge, but contrary to popular myth, medical fees for injured foreign runners are not covered by the town council. Years ago some foreigners, most notably Noel Chandler, began hosting breakfasts after the encierro where one could nurse any injuries they may have received in the running that morning or in romance the night before, and these gatherings began to be called enfermerías.

Entrada: A ticket. Used here it refers to a ticket for the bullfight. The scalper's cry of "Hay entradas, sol y sombra" or "I have tickets for sale, both in the sun and shade" is often heard near a Spanish bullring just before a major corrida. In Pamplona the scalpers approach more secretively and quietly as the practice is illegal. The price of a seat is determined by its location; its height or distance from the sand; and whether it is in the shade, the sun, or sol y sombra, which refers to those seats which are in the sun when the bullfight begins and in the shade when it ends.

Faena: The penultimate portion of a bullfight, when the matador works the bull with the muleta, a small serge cloth, just before the kill. It is at this point that the matador, who first faced the bull alone with a large cape, now stands before the bull alone again, armed only with a small red cloth and sword. The truth of the corrida is articulated in these ten minutes between the dedication of the bull and its death.

Faja: The red loosely knotted sash worn around the waist by all during fiesta in Pamplona, the south of Navarra and parts of Aragón. Though the 1889 poster features a horseman with a red sash and the 1921 cartel depicts a drummer wearing a faja, its adoption by Fiesta-goers at large was gradual, beginning in the 1930s after the Spanish Civil War.

Feria: Literally, a fair such as a county fair. The Fiesta as we know it today grows out of and was once linked to an ancient medieval fair held in Pamplona beginning on midsummer's eve and running for three weeks, and a later trade fair of longer duration. Today the words feria and fiesta are often used interchangeably.

Festivale: In this book, the term refers to a bullfight that does not conform to the standard format of three full matadors and their cuadrillas facing six fighting bulls raised on the same ranch. Festivales can involve rejoneadores who fight on horseback; six bulls from six separate ranches; two matadors facing three bulls each in a mano a mano, one matador fighting six bulls, and other combinations that vary from the format of a formal corrida de toros or bullfight.

Fiesta: Literally, feast, as in the Feast of St. Stephen. Originally the word had a purely religious connotation but now it is synonymous with most large street festivals in Spain.

Figuras: Here the term applies to retired matadors who have achieved an elevated status, men remembered long after the era in which they were active, as well as to those active matadors thought to possess the skill, talent and gifts that will enable them to continue to be considered figuras long after their time. These matadors, however, are not to be confused with phenomenons of the bullring, matadors who flash like comets across the taurine sky from time to time making a huge noise and trailing a bright light, making no impact and leaving no lasting imprint.

Ganadero: One who raises toro bravos or fighting bulls. Breeding properties are often in the hands of very wealthy families whose source of financial strength comes from other commercial endeavors. This is not to say that raising fighting bulls is ever a hobby, sideline or pastime. It is a serious endeavor. When the young, two-year-old vacas, or cows, are tested on a ranch, the ganadero seated in the palco, a balcony above the small bullring, will hold "the book" in his lap. In this book he or she can trace the lineage of the young vacas back many generations.

Gigantes: The giants of Fiesta, eight larger-than-life figures created in the mid-1800s by a local Navarran artist, Tadeo Amorena. The Gigantes represent the mythical kings and queens of Europe, Asia, Africa and America. Beautifully dressed in lace and satin they appear to dance thanks to the strong, nimble men who carry the 130-pound statues using internal harnesses. The Gigantes are popular with small children and they begin their procession through the city at 9:30 a.m. each day. The first memory of Sanfermines for most people born in Pamplona is of the Gigantes. Each year the men who carry the Gigantes have a banquet toward the end of Fiesta, and in front of their place settings is a small replica of the Gigante they have carried all week. Seated next to these men are their fathers and grandfathers who carried the figure in their day.

    In ancient times very different kinds of figures paraded through Fiesta, giants representing horrors such as pestilence, famine and war. These figures were tossed into a huge bonfire at the end of the celebration in hopes that these things would not be visited on the populace during the year ahead.

Gored/Goring: Where the bull's sharp horn pierces the skin and enters the body of a torero or bullrunner. Known in Spanish as a cornada, this is distinct from a cogida or more minor wound or other injuries which can be inflicted by a run-in with a toro bravo. A goring is often life threatening while other injuries are likely less grave, though the immense power of a fighting bull is such that a tossing in either the bullfight or the street can permanently paralyze a torero or runner.

Grada: The highest tier of the bullring and the cheapest seats in the house. Ticket prices rise according to how close you are to the sand and whether or not your seat is in sun or shade. Many foreigners in Pamplona wish to sit in the shade near the sand, while many locals would not consider a seat that was not in the sun among the raucous peñas.

Iruña: The Basque name for Pamplona (also spelled Iruñea), which literally translates as "the city." Also the name of the large and ornate café and bar on the Plaza del Castillo favored by American writer Ernest Hemingway.

In medieval times Basques were concentrated near the cathedral, in the area known as La Navarrería. Estafeta, which is the longest street on the bullrun, was the center of the Jewish Quarter. The Frankish King Roland sacked Iruña in 778 and was then ambushed at the Roncesvalles Pass, not by Arabs as in the legend of "The Song of Roland," but by Basques bent on revenge for his act of pillage.

Jota: A short folksong native to southern Navarra, Aragón and the Rioja region sung sometimes in groups with a guitar and sometimes a capella. The theme of a jota usually concerns love or longing for your home, and a jota can also have a religious theme. Recent jotas address social issues such as the drought in southern Navarra. The towns of Artajona in Navarra and Calahorra in the Rioja are famous for their jota singers, but Pamplona has its share. Also a folk dance done with hands held above the head, palms skyward, and feet moving in a criss-crossing manner.

Kaiku: A local brand of vanilla or chocolate-flavored milk often mixed with cheap cognac and served with ice on a hot day or steamed when the weather turns inclement.

Kalimoxto: (pronounced "kali-moe-choe") A mixture of red wine and Coca-Cola served over ice with a slice of lemon drunk primarily by young people. The exact origins of this bizarre cocktail are unknown but it is rumored to have been invented in the late '70s by locals searching for a drink that was refreshing, alcoholic and cheap. The caffeine aids endurance, and this is a good "pacing" beverage due to its relatively low alcoholic content. Today some bars have a Coke tap next to a tap dispensing cheap red wine or even a combined kalimotxo tap. Often served in one-liter plastic cups called cachi-cachis.

Manada: A herd of fighting bulls.

Mano a mano: A bullfight in which two matadors compete "hand to hand," each fighting three bulls of six from the same ranch.

Matador: A professional bullfighter; literally, "killer." Everyone who wears a suit of lights is properly called a torero, including picadors and banderilleros. Only a matador wears gold on his traje de luces or suit of lights, and only a matador kills the bull.

Merienda: A picnic or mid-afternoon snack; during Sanfermines this term refers to the meal eaten in the plaza de toros at around 7:30 p.m. after the third bull has been dragged out. Generally speaking, the cheaper the seats, the larger the merienda. This meal can consist of something as simple as a large ham sandwich but many of the peñas and large family groups bring pans filled with serrano ham and tomatoes, cod stew, braised bull meat and rich desserts to consume either while watching the rest of the bullfight or in the open passageways behind the stands. The food is often washed down with sangría brought in newly purchased plastic garbage cans of all sizes.

Montón: Literally, mountain; a pileup of fallen bullrunners caused by runners tripping over each other in a confined space such as the entrance to the bullring. A bull's instinct is to jump over rather than go through a large mass of bodies which present an obstacle to following the rest of the herd. In a montón the bulls and runners can get tangled up together. A young runner who was never even touched by a bull was tragically crushed to death in a montón in front of the plaza de toros in 1977. Changes in the positioning of the barricades, the creation of ground-level cutouts in the callejón or tunnel to allow downed runners to roll to safety and other minor changes have decreased the frequency and size of montónes, though the potential for a massive pileup is ever-present.

Morrillo: The uppermost part of the humped muscle on the back of a bull's neck. When a bull is enraged, his morrillo is raised and firm, and it is the target of the tip of the picador's lance. In the encierro, sometimes the last bulls may come up the street alone, having slipped and been left behind. An experienced runner seeing a lone or loose bull called a suelto immediately looks to the morrillo as an indicator of whether the animal is enraged and looking to attack or simply exhausted and looking for the way home.

Mozo: A local word, rarely used outside Navarra and Aragón, for a young person. During Sanfermines it refers to young people in the street participating in Fiesta or the encierro.

Mozo de espadas: A matador's sword handler who also helps him dress for the bullfight and assists him during the corrida offstage, behind the barrera or wall separating him from the sand. He is an essential member of the cuadrilla and the only one who does not wear a suit of lights. Usually a mozo de espadas is in comfortable clothes for he functions as the equipment manager. Helping to dress the matador is an important function, but the hardest part of his work comes after the corrida. As others repair to a bar or restaurant, the mozo may work late into the night, removing blood stains from clothing, capes and muletas.

1909 Cartel

Muleta: The small red serge cloth used by the matador in the faena, the final third of the bullfight. Unlike the large cape or capote which is one color on one side and a different color on the other and is used in the first two acts of the drama, the muleta has always been solid red on both sides. Hence the old saying about "a bull seeing red." The animals are actually color blind.

Naturales: Passes made with the muleta held in the matador's left hand. Naturales are perhaps the most beautiful and difficult passes made during the faena for in these passes the cloth hangs from just a stick and is not supported by or fanned to a larger shape by the sword as it is during right hand passes. This smaller target can produce a visual elegance rarely equalled by right hand passes. The reputations of many matadors are made with the left hand, and similarly there is sometimes criticism that a bullfighter is a bit too right-handed.

Navarra: The Spanish province of which Pamplona is the capital city and seat of regional government. Navarra was an ancient independent kingdom that stretched north across the Pyrenees into France. Established in 818 when Iñigo Iñiguez was crowned King, Navarra remained independent until 1512 when most of the kingdom was incorporated into the Spanish crown and the northern territory beyond the mountains was claimed by France. Navarra played a key role in the re-conquest of the Iberian Peninsula from the armies of Islam. Even after its incorporation into Spain, Navarra retained many regional rights and privileges known as los fueros, and special fiscal powers. To the present day Navarra uses a slightly different legal code from the rest of Spain.

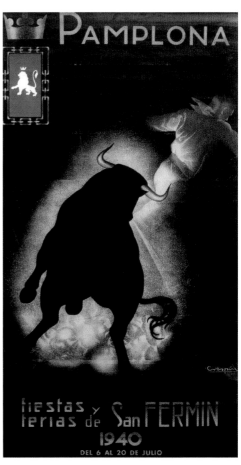

Noble y bravo: Noble and brave. Refers to a bull with good casta or breeding, an animal willing to charge bravely and forthrightly, repeating charges on command, maintaining its strength in the face of punishment, and rising to the challenge of the corrida. Also a phrase used to describe Navarran bullrunners who run in the same manner in which great bulls fight, men who rise to the challenge and perform with bravery and honor.

Padrino: Godfather, but also the senior bullfighter who sponsors a young matador making his alternativa. This is a title taken seriously in taurine circles and even more seriously among Navarrans asked to serve as padrino for the child of a relative or friend.

1940 Cartel

Paella: A saffron rice dish that usually includes seafood, meat and vegetables. Indigenous to Valencia and Andalucía but now eaten across Spain.

La Pamplonesa: The semi-professional town hall band that starts the day's festivities at 6:45 a.m. with dianas and plays throughout Fiesta.

Pancarta: Literally, banner, but usually taken to mean the banners which are carried aloft in front of peña bands on their way to and from the bullfight. Each banner carries a different cartoon dealing with contemporary local issues in a sometimes scandalous and at times libelous manner. In the days of strict censorship under the Franco regime, the peña banners were one of the few outlets for political satire in the entire country.

Pañuelo: A neckerchief, almost always red, worn from midday July 6 until the close of Fiesta at midnight July 14. At the opening of Fiesta these kerchiefs are held aloft in two hands by all who chant the saint's name. When the rocket fires, pandemonium erupts and the pañuelo is tied around the neck. At the closing ceremony, when midnight strikes and a rocket fires, the pañuelo is removed and placed in a pocket. Some carry their pañuelos to the church of San Lorenzo after the final ceremony and tie them to a large iron gate, and others tie their pañuelos and sashes to lampposts as they head home.

Parador: A state-regulated, top-class hotel often situated in a national monument or overlooking a geographic wonder.

Paseo: The formal entrance into the bullring in which the matadors and their cuadrillas parade across the sand, salute the president and take up their places for the entrance of the first bull.

Pasodobles: Dramatic music written for the bullfight by some of Spain's greatest composers. Some of these pieces carry the names of great matadors past and present. When the final part of the fight is proceeding artistically, the musical director will call for the band to play a pasodoble. The music heightens one's emotional response to the art.

Pastores: Literally, shepherds, but also ranch hands who accompany toro bravos from the ranch to the bullring. In Pamplona pastores are spread along the entire route of the encierro. The lives they have saved cannot be counted, and many whose lives are saved by them are unaware of their presence. Armed only with a long cane stick, a knowledge of bulls second to none and great courage, these men insure the bulls move safely up the street. When a runner is doing something stupid and endangering himself, others or impeding the progress of moving a suelto or solo bull up the street, a pastor will turn the stick on him to get him out of the way or freeze him so he can complete his job with the bull.

Patio de caballos: The area of the bullring where the picadors' horses are exercised and where aficionados and toreros gather before the fight. This is also where the butchering area was located when bulls were butchered on site. The emergency operating room and the chapel where matadors pray before a corrida are usually located in or near the area of the patio de caballos.

Peñas: Social clubs originally formed in the mid-nineteenth century by groups of young men dedicated to celebrating the Sanfermines. The first, "El Trueno" (The Thunder), was formed in 1852 but no longer exists. Women were originally barred from membership but this is no longer the case. At least one woman has held the title of president of a peña. The clubs are financed by their membership and a grant from the town council. Each peña has its own marching band and clubhouse from which it organizes social activities throughout the year. Fiesta, however, is the main focus of the peñas.

Pensión: A cheap boarding house one grade below a hostel; often part of a family home. During Sanfermines there is no such thing as cheap accommodations as demand easily outstrips supply. Many Fiesta fanatics from across the world reserve the same room year after year. Rooms in Pamplona pensiónes are easier to obtain mid-week and nearly impossible to secure on weekends.

Picadors: Toreros on horseback armed with a long pole that has a spear-like steel tip at the end. Driving the pica into the charging bull's neck muscles weakens the animal and causes it to lower its head in preparation for the next stage of the bullfight. Pic-ing also fulfills the bull, allowing it to strike a combatant with the full force of its horns and body.

Plaza: A square or public area in a town or city. In Pamplona there are many squares that are active during Fiesta. The main square is Plaza del Castillo. A more curious square bounded by beautiful buildings is Plaza de San Francisco. In every depiction one sees of St. Francis of Assisi, the saint is shown with little birds and tiny animals like rabbits and squirrels, though there is no evidence the man had any affinity for animals. The Navarran St. Francis is a macho saint, depicted not with a little rabbit but with a full-grown wolf.

Plaza de toros: Bullring. Pamplona's is run by a Catholic charity, the Casa de Misericordia in Pamplona, which cares for the elderly. Abonos, season tickets, are dispensed from an office at the old folks home close to the funfair. Profits from the bullfights are plowed back into care for the elderly.

Quite: (pronounced "Kee-tay") A movement by a torero with a cape to lure the bull away from a picador's horse or to save a downed colleague following a fall or spill in the ring.

Rejoneador: A mounted bullfighter; a highly skilled rider who places banderillas from horseback and usually descends to fight and kill the bull on foot. Bullfighting on the Iberian Peninsula began as a spectacle on horseback. Originally the men who engaged in the activity were members of the wealthy nobility class. Little has changed in that regard for a string of horses owned by a rejoneador can easily exceed a million dollars in value. Bullfighting on foot dates only from the late eighteenth century and for a long time was a poor boy's only shot at money and glory.

1945 *Cartel*

San Fermín: St. Fermín, the patron saint of Pamplona in whose honor the Fiesta is held. He and San Francisco Javier are the co-patrons of Navarra. San Fermín's effigy is brought out of the San Lorenzo church at 10:30 a.m. July 7 and it is followed by a solemn and dignified procession of the town council dressed in ceremonial garb, clergymen, the bishop of Pamplona and local townsfolk.

Fermín was born in Pamplona in the fifth century, the son of a Roman senator who had converted to Christianity. An archbishop at 24, Fermín traveled north to Amiens in pagan Gaul when he was 31 years old and he was martyred there by decapitation. A fragment of his skull was brought to Pamplona in January 1186 and venerated as a sacred relic. The first religious services in his honor date from that time. Pamplona's attachment to the saint grew over the following centuries and the last holy relic was brought from Amiens in 1941. San Fermín is also the patron saint of Amiens and Lesaka, a small market town in northern Navarra, which holds a quieter fiesta on the same dates each year.

Sanfermines: The name of the Fiesta, which runs from July 6-14.

Fiesta originally began on October 10, the anniversary of the establishment of San Fermín's mission in Amiens. Little evidence of the earliest fiestas exists, but by the late fourteenth century we see accounts of bullfights, communal meals and jousts accompanying the religious devotion to the saint.

In 1690, after several years of bad fall weather, the Pamplona town council petitioned the ecclesiastical courts to have the feast day changed to July 7. That date has no religious significance or relation to Fermín's life and death: the people just wanted to enjoy better weather and follow the markets and fairs celebrated from midsummer's night, June 21. This petition was approved and the first summer Sanfermines was celebrated in 1691. In earlier centuries the dates were less specific and Fiesta sometimes extended until July 20.

Shampú: A colloquial expression for champagne or sparkling wine. Champagne mixed with lemon or lemon sorbet has become a mainstay in Pamplona.

Siesta: A nap usually taken after lunch and before the bullfight. However, in Fiesta you will often see people grabbing a siesta at any time of the day or night on benches, in parks or slumped over tables.

Sorteo: The actual allocating of bulls at the apartado, when the bulls are divided into lots and the cuadrillas' representatives draw for them.

Suelto: A loose bull in the encierro, a toro bravo which has become separated from the herd and is consequently much more dangerous as it is more likely to attack.

Suerte: Luck. Bullrunners wish one another "buena suerte" in the minutes before the rocket. In the corrida this word of the same spelling and pronunciation has several meanings, including a reference to the acts of the spectacle as in "suerte de banderillas."

Tapas: Small portions of food, usually enclosed in glass, displayed on the top of bars appearing between 11 a.m. and 2 p.m. and then again around 7 p.m. The range of bar food offered is not as extensive during Sanfermines as it is during the rest of the year. An honesty system is often in operation with the barkeep trusting the customer to tell him how many snacks have been consumed when the bill is settled. Cheats beware: Pamplona waiters may look drunk, but they have excellent memories and keen eyes. Tapas are also called banderillas when they are skewered on toothpicks.

Temporada: The bullfight season usually stretching from March to October. Technically, most still consider the opening in February at Castellón de la Plana on the Mediterranean. There are occasionally special corridas and charity events fought during the winter months in southern Spain.

Tendido: Refers to the lower tiers of the bullring and the seats closest to the sand.

Torero: Anyone involved in the corrida who is attired in a traje de luces, which includes the matador, picador and banderillero.

Toril: The door through which a bull enters the ring.

Toro: A bull.

Toro bravo: Technically, in terms of toreo or bullfighting, the words translate to "wild bull" referring to its untamed or non-domesticated state. Often, English language writers refer to the word bravo as meaning brave which is also a characteristic of the fighting bull that appears in a corrida, a breed not closely related in terms of its instincts and temperament to the domesticated livestock found in other parts of the world. A toro bravo's physical characteristics are equally distinct and even an untrained eye can observe an Andalucian herd grazing from a long distance and know whether they are beef cattle or toro bravos. The vacas or cows of this breed, for instance, would likely use their stiletto sharp horns to gore to death a person attempting to milk one of them. In fact, it is believed the courage in the breed comes from the females and it is usually only the young cows who are tested in their second year to determine their suitability as breeding stock. It has been suggested by more than one person that perhaps true courage resides in the females of all species, including humans.

Traje de luces: "Suit of lights," the glimmering sequined costume worn by a torero. The suits are heavy and fitted tightly. Entire books have been devoted to the subject of the development, design and tailoring of these elaborate suits. Trajes provide no protection and are so heavy and tight that most would have difficulty walking normally while wearing one. They are part of the tradition, and the price of one good traje made by a taurine tailor in Madrid or Sevilla can easily exceed three thousand U.S. dollars and sometimes cost a great deal more. A top matador will have many trajes.

Tremendista: A term used to describe a flashy or showy bullfighter whose repertoire is filled with what most aficionados consider tricks that have little to do with the art of toreo. Some tremendista bullfighters are unnecessarily or even insanely brave, and they have their following. Their use of adornos and other unnecessary stunts can be great crowd pleasers, which offers more of a commentary on the tastes of a particular crowd than an endorsement of the matador's ability, for few tremendistas are ever applauded and accepted by critics and serious aficionados.

Txistu: (pronounced "chis-too") A small musical instrument about the size of a flute or piccolo that sounds out as a reed instrument and is played on the move in a marching cadence. Accomplished players simultaneously rattle out one-handed rolls on a snare drum as they march along.

Vacas: In this usage, it refers to cows born of the breed of fighting bulls. Vacas are aggressive. Young vacas are let loose in the bullring after the encierro is over and the bulls and cabestros are safely in their pens. The vacas' horns are sometimes sheathed in leather during this event, though they sometimes race around the bullring with their sharp horns flashing. Young men and women try their skill "running the vacas," entertaining the crowd assembled in the plaza de toros.

Valientes: "The brave ones," the ironic term given to terrified bull runners who reach the bullring several minutes in advance of the first bull. They may return home to tell anyone who will listen that they "ran the bulls in Pamplona" and in their minds they probably did.

Verónicas: Cape passes executed by a matador during the first third of the bullfight and named for St. Veronica, who wiped the sweat and blood from Christ's face as he carried the cross toward Calvary. A verónica is initiated when the cape is spread widely to receive the charge and remains extended as the bull moves past the matador. When half the cape is pulled behind the torero's body in a media verónica, the pass becomes more dramatic.

Vespers: The religious evening service held on July 6 in the presence of the full town council at the San Lorenzo church which holds the relics of San Fermín. In past centuries this was the first act of the Sanfermines. Vespers are sung by a local choir with an international reputation. The group practices year round, records albums, and performs in foreign countries. Their recordings include religious music of the Pamplona cathedral dating to the fifteenth century.

BUILDING THE BOOK:
The Process and the People

T O TAKE ONE GOOD PHOTOGRAPH of the encierro, a photographer leaves their hotel before sunrise in order to stake out a position along the half-mile course. The position chosen depends on a lot of variables. The day of the week is a determinate of what the crowding conditions will be. The surface of the street affects the footing of men and animals alike. Some breeds of bulls generally run the course in a tight pack, others are typically strung out. Weather conditions, especially cloud cover and its affect on available light in some sections of the shaded course, are a factor. After placing oneself in the best possible position, there still are no guarantees that one will make a good image. The encierro images that exist in this book depict a field of action that existed but for a micro-second.

It has often been written that the bullfight is an art form which simply does not transmit to film, for the emotion of the corrida is not something that can be lifted from the sand and printed on paper. The corrida as seen through the lens of a photographer must be viewed with the eyes of one who either has an in-depth knowledge of bullfighting, or by a photographer who possesses a deep appreciation of other art forms and can transfer their artistic sensibility to the bullring. Making pictures that convey the beauty, brutality, grace and art of the spectacle, images that transmit the emotion of a bullfight, is an even more difficult challenge than getting a good encierro picture.

The Fiesta itself rolls around town, careening all day and all night on its own schedule with unpredictability as its hallmark. At times fiesta is a rowdy, surrealistic scene, and at other times it presents a soft, sweet sentimental picture. To bring the essence of the fiesta out of Pamplona onto the pages of a book through images, to harness the true core spirit of Pamplona's celebration and transmit same to an audience through photographs requires something far beyond the technical expertise of a professional photographer. It requires an understanding of what surrounds the photographer - the people, places and things of fiesta. To make pictures that depict not only the action of fiesta, but also portray and reflect the mood of the event, requires tireless devotion.

JOANNA PINNEO has an international reputation. A Pulitzer nominee and winner of the Alfred Eisenstaedt Award, she worked in Pamplona as part of an assignment for  *National Geographic* in the Basque country. She has worked in over 65 countries during her twenty year career. The list of her accomplishments, awards, articles and exhibitions fills pages. An even longer list is that of publications such as *Life, New York Times Magazine, Time, Geo, Stern, U.S. News & World Report, Mother Jones and American Photographer*, among others. Pinneo's career is characterized by a respectful portrayal of humanity and dignity of people around the world. The project that she has sustained a passionate interest in for years, a work in progress, is an extensive photo essay on girls of all backgrounds coming of age in America. She is represented by the Aurora and Quanta Productions Photo Agency in Maine. Joanna and her husband, Walt, live in the Rocky Mountains.

DESMOND BOYLAN won the Concurso Periodístico Internacional San  Fermín for best photograph in Pamplona in 1998 for the picture on page 34, an image of a bull picking up two runners, one on each horn. The image ranks as one of the all-time greatest encierro pictures.

Obviously the green shirt hooked with the right horn had to have torn free immediately after the image was made and the bull would have shucked the runner off his left horn just as quickly. The scene we see in the frame existed for a millisecond. This photograph, the cover of this book, and first two fiesta images in this book, with all other Boylan photos contained herein are a fair representation of his talent. A twelve year veteran of Fiesta, Boylan finds the chaos of Pamplona a respite from other assignments where he often finds himself covering wars for Reuters from the side receiving incoming shelling and bombing. In 1999 he covered the bombardment of Yugoslavia on the incoming side, from Belgrade, having bombs dropped around him for three months, and he has covered the Mid-East conflict since 1994, as well as working assignments for Reuters in other embattled places like Albania, Bosnia, Serbia, Algeria, Lybia, and Lebanon. Desmond met and married his wife, Gloria, in Cuba and they live with their son, Michael, in Madrid.

SANTIAGO LYON, Chief of Photography for the Associated Press in Madrid, has a long relationship with Sanfermines. Santi was in fiesta with his father, then the chief bullfight critic for a Madrid daily, when he was a young boy. Lyon has covered conflicts and photographed combat in El Salvador, Panama, the Gulf War,  Croatia, Yemen, Albania,  Kosovo and Afghanistan and Bosnia. Though he has been under fire, seriously wounded, captured and detained by a foreign army, Lyon says running with the Miura bulls in Pamplona was the most terrifying experience of his life. Santiago first met writer-photographer EMMA DALY while she was working as a foreign correspondent in Central America covering fighting and human rights issues. Later the two of them covered the Balkans where Daly traveled widely and reported from all three sides of the conflict. She has worked for a number of publications, including *Newsweek, The Observer* and *Conde Nast Traveler*. Today Emma Daly writes for *The New York Times*. Emma and Santi are married and have a daughter, Sara Alexandra, a young lady whose arrival into the world was cheered by a legion of her parents friends in Pamplona as her birth was announced via cell phone to a large group in fiesta on July 9, 2001.

JOHN KIMMICH-JAVIER is a fiery, committed, tireless shooter who is everywhere in fiesta every summer, while he serves as a professor at the University of Iowa the balance of the year.  For two decades Kimmich-Javier has been traveling internationally and photographing extensively, with a primary interest in his Hispanic roots. His travels have taken him from the Pre-Columbian cultures in Central America to the Iberian and Moorish cultures of Spain. His list of foreign assignments, exhibitions and permanent collections housing his work in North America and Europe is a long one. His many awards include first prize in the National Photographers Association Picture of the year competition for bullfight and bullrunning photographs. His wife, Swedish born journalist Maria Nilsson, works with him on free-lance projects. As he shoots primarily in black & white and this project is all color, except for historic images, only a glimpse of his talent is showcased here, but undoubtedly there will be a full volume of his Pamplona work available in time. A retrospective exhibition of his fiesta photographs was mounted in Pamplona in 2001. He is represented internationally by the picture agency Bildhuset, Stockholm, and in the U.S. by ArchiTech Gallery, Chicago.

GERRY DAWES, a writer-photographer, contributed photographs of individual Americans for this book. However, the images are but a small sampling of his work in progress, a lengthy project in which he has invested heart and soul for years, "Homage To Iberia: More Travels and Reflections." This work carries the endorsement of and a foreword by James Michener, the man who wrote the original *Iberia*.

The work traces Michener's steps across the Iberian peninsula and draws on Dawes' thirty plus years experience in Spain, his acquired expertise in many aspects of the diverse provinces of the country, as well as his relationship with the people mentioned in *Iberia* and their descendants. Dawes knows bullfighting well and is an authority  on the gastronomy, wines, and culture of Spain. His work has appeared in a wide array of publications such as *The Berlitz Travelers Guide to Spain, Martha Stewart Living,* and *The New York Times,* and he also has worked as a consultant for film and television projects like the CBS program *60 Minutes.*

Z. ABDULLAH made a long journey from his homeland to Pamplona. Born Zaheeruddin Abdullah in Afghanistan, he grew up to be imprisoned and tortured three times under different regimes. During the  Russian war he was placed in prison, and later the Taliban tortured him and finally Al Qaeda detained him when he was photographing damage done by U.S. missiles in the retaliatory attack after the bombing of the embassies in Africa. A free-lance photographer who has worked for major media concerns around the globe and had his work honored at the annual international conclave of professional photographers in Perpignan, France, Abdullah was granted political asylum in Spain after he escaped Afghanistan. When the U.S. military action commenced in Afghanistan, Abdullah went back to his homeland as a photo-journalist. After years of waiting, his wife and children were able to leave Afghanistan and join him in Europe. In Pamplona, Abdullah is seemingly known to everyone, a very popular character who enjoys the fiesta full out.

Other images in this book were made by: Joe Riehl, an author who has written scholarly books as well as plays while teaching

English at The University of Louisiana-Lafayette and pursuing a myriad of other interests extending to photography and film-making; Melony Barrios Mouton, who works with her husband on projects like this one and returns often to the Quintana Roo region of Mexico where she pursues a photo essay of the province; and Robert Strauss, a professional photographer who works in New York; Ton Van der Berg, a graphic artist and photographer in the Netherlands; Janis Heymann, a painter in Louisiana; and Edward Gans, an assistant professor of communications at Linfield College in Oregon where he resides with his wife, Lisa; and Elizabeth Stallworth, an architect who works on housing for the disadvantaged and resides with her husband Jeff and son Grant in Alabama. The stunning sequence of the "Riley roll-around" at pages 164 and 165 appears courtesy of Zubieta y Retegui, one of the oldest, most respected photography businesses in Pamplona. The entire visual history of the encierro is contained in their archives.

The photographers referenced above submitted over five hundred photographs in varying formats: prints, transparencies, digital images on disc, and others forwarded via the Internet. These images combined with an original manuscript exceeding 75,000 words comprised the raw material from which this book was built.

To fashion a coherent volume from all this material, integrating the work of many different contributors, creating a work that remained faithful in its final context to the individual conceptual aims of all the artists involved, fell upon the shoulders of Megan Barra, an independent graphic designer, art director and artist. Megan Barra has won so many awards for her work in a variety of media that she no longer lists them on her curriculum vitae. In January 2002 it was announced that Barra was named as one of five Grammy nominees for Best Recording Package for the design of Sonny Landreth's *Levee Town* release on Sugar Hill Records.

Megan's process begins with immersion. She searches the subject matter in an effort to find the right tone and feel for the design. With this project, she immersed herself in independent research on the subjects of this book, including the colors and music of Spain in general and fiesta specifically. For nearly a year this designer who has been named Art Director of the Year seven times by the Advertising Federation she belongs to, devoted herself to developing this material into the form in which it appears today. This project went through countless phases of design and redesign as Megan Barra poured herself into the book, always pressing to get the right tone and feel. Every detail from the hand-lettered fonts she created for title pages to the placement of each photograph was carefully considered and reconsidered by Barra again and again as she patiently assembled this book line by line, page by page. The result here is apparent and equally beautiful are other designs of Barra's that have appeared in publications of The Art Directors Club of New York, Graphis Book Design, The Society of Illustrators Annual, and the American Advertising Federation. Her original artwork and limited editions of reproductions of her art have sold out within a few days of being offered for sale. Megan lives in Lafayette, Louisiana and is well-versed in the culture, especially the music, of this place she calls home.

While Megan Barra worked on the design and artistic direction and composition of the volume, Todd Mouton tackled the big manuscript and cut it down to size, making tough editing decisions word by word. Mouton, a free-lance writer who has covered Louisiana music extensively, works for the Acadiana Arts Council. He has collaborated with Megan Barra on a number of projects prior to working with her on this book. He has been to Fiesta a number of times, most recently with his wife Jen, his partner in Bayou Booking and Management, a music business and booking company. They live in rural St. Martin Parish, Louisiana.

ACKNOWLEDGMENTS

AMES MICHENER'S *Iberia* caused me to travel to Pamplona. I was intrigued by Sanfermines and two expatriates he wrote about who were later to become friends of mine, John Fulton and Matt Carney. Near the end of Michener's life we spent a Sunday in Austin talking about those extraordinary men and Fiesta. A circle closed in Texas, something begun thirty years earlier. These three men, Matt Carney, John Fulton and Jim Michener who were so closely associated with fiesta, were strangers to me in the beginning, just people mentioned on the pages of a big book. In the end, they were my friends. The words I need to express my debt to all three of them for all they shared with me are words only a poet would know. My hope is that this book honors their memory.

The feelings I have about what Bob Jones contributed are just as hard to express. A true patron of the arts and adventurer who loves Fiesta, Bob believed enough in this book to extend himself in an act of extraordinary kindness and uncommon generosity, furnishing all that was needed to make it a reality. Joining him as publisher is Quinn Jones who has also run the bulls and bars of Pamplona. Their support of this project has been of monumental importance.

I know this book first began to take shape when it was entrusted to the hands of readers who made it better with each suggestion, and they are Angus MacSwan, Jesse Graham, Tom Gowen, and Joe Riehl. The debt I owe them is equaled by the indebtedness I feel toward Janis Heymann who did the original art direction, the painstaking work of assembling a mockup of the first version of the book that brought out the potential in the project.

The book was finally shaped by Todd Mouton who worked as copy editor on every version and revision, did fact checking, and functioned as project consultant and graphic designer liaison, and participated in editing over five hundred photographs. Through the process, he worked tirelessly and he argued a lot with his father. Fortunately, he won all the important rounds.

The photographers who contributed to this project with images made during long days and nights in Pamplona, people whose credentials are on a foregoing page, give this volume texture, depth, and art. This is their book too.

The images of Pamplona cartels appear courtesy of Ayuntamiento de Pamplona as they graciously granted permission to us to share this artwork.

Paul Bower, Mark Oldfield and Chris Williams contributed as much to the drinking passages in an informational sense as they have over the years to Pamplona bars in a financial sense. Their sense of the history, customs and traditions of Fiesta were of immense value in constructing a glossary that is not only accurate and informative, but in some instances reflective of their humor.

A lot of this book was written in a wonderful setting among people who have become family over the years at a small hotel on the Mediterranean in southern France. To the two named Sheona and the two named Robert, and Sandi, those who gave us the keys to the hotel kitchen and anything else we needed, we owe a lot.

The most important acknowledgment, my deepest gratitude is owed to Megan Barra, an artist and art director who is capable of making art out of chaos. One of the happiest days of my life was the day that Megan agreed to take on the project and "build this book." In the end, this book is as much Megan Barra's as it is the photographer's or writer's, and probably more so.

Every writer thanks their family, none more sincerely than I. My wife, Melony, did some heavy lifting in the proofing and editing area, and argued punctuation with me all the way. She believed in the book more than anyone. Todd and Matt worked hands-on, Chad educated me about the Internet, and Jeanne' always extended love and support, and gave me popsicles.

DIRECTORY

Publisher
Quinn Publishing
2424 Edenborn Avenue, Suite 216
Metairie, LA 70001
E-Mail: quinnpub@bellsouth.net

Author
Ray Mouton
1000 Bourbon Street, No. 206
New Orleans, LA 70116
E-Mail: RayMouton@aol.com

Designer
Megan Barra Graphic Design
PO Box 51403
Lafayette, LA 70505

Photographers
Joanna B. Pinneo
member of
Aurora and Quanta Productions, Inc
188 State St, Suite 300
Portland, ME 04101
Tel: 207.828.8787
Fax: 207.828.5524
www.auroraphotos.com
www.grrlstories.org

Desmond Boylan
Calle Molino de Viento 8, 3 Ext Dcha
28004 Madrid
Spain
E-Mail dboylan@terra.es

Santiago Lyon/Emma Daly
Plaza del Dos de Mayo 9 - 6 izq.
28004 Madrid
Spain

Gerry Dawes
17 Charnwood Drive - Suite A
Suffern, NY 10901 USA
Tel: 845.368.3486
Fax: 845.357.6093
Cellular Phone: 914.414.6982
E-Mail: gerrydawes@aol.com